SPICE

SO-ATD-550

Suggested Activities to Motivate the Teaching of the Language Arts

Mary E. Platts
Sherman Oaks, California

Sr. Rose Marguerite, s.g.c.
Principal, St. Joseph Convent
Haverhill, Massachusetts

Esther Shumaker
Elementary Teacher
Albuquerque, New Mexico

EDUCATIONAL SERVICE, INC.
P. O. Box 219
Stevensville, Michigan 49127

Games 99-174

TABLE OF CONTENTS

INDEX

TEACHING THE CONSONANTS
Seatwork Activities

Games

Independent Work Activities

TEACHING THE VOWELS
Seatwork Activities

Games

Independent Work Activities

TEACHING THE THREE-LETTER WORDS

Seatwork Activities

Games

Independent Work Activities

TEACHING THE BLEND WORDS

Seatwork Activities

Games

Independent Work Activities

TEACHING THE LETTER COMBINATIONS
Seatwork Activities

Games

Independent Work Activities

Games

READING FOR MEANING

Seatwork Activities

Games

Independent Work Activities

CREATIVE WRITING

Seatwork Activities

Games

Independent Work Activities

MISCELLANEOUS

Seatwork Activities

Games

Independent Work Activities

INTRODUCTION

Spice, as its name implies, is intended to add new zest and flavor to the language arts program. It cannot, of course, replace the "main diet" of a developmental, sequential language arts program, nor the necessary drills in subject matter. But the activities presented here can give children incentive for, and practice in, the skills and understandings presented in the language arts program.

As teachers, we see long-range educational goals for our children, and see each day's work as another step in the cumulative process necessary to achieve these goals. But children live in the present. It is hard for them to comprehend these future needs for which we are preparing them. They need "right now" goals, and immediate opportunities to put their new learnings into practice.

The idea of using activities in the classroom was first developed by John Dewey as a result of his experience in his Activity School. He concluded that when children were able to put their learnings to immediate and realistic use, their logical understanding, retention, and ability to put into practice these learnings, were greatly increased. It is upon this basic philosophy that this text was developed.

Consider the difference in child-response to these two methods of introducing new phonetic material:

1. "Today we are going to learn three new sounds. They are 'ack,' 'ick,' and 'ock.'" (The teacher then proceeds with the lesson.)

2. "I have a new puzzle for you today. (The teacher shows the puzzle to the class, perhaps tells how it is to be worked, and children comment on

-1-

it.) As you noticed, this puzzle has some new sounds. They are 'ack,' 'ick,' and 'ock.' You will want to listen carefully as we talk about these sounds so you will be able to work the puzzle after the phonics lesson."

Notice that the activity did not replace the formal phonics lesson; it merely added interest and incentive (or, as we term it, "spice"). And, of course, the activity itself will give an opportunity to practice and apply the new learnings — thus a two-fold gain by the addition of the activity, and certainly no loss of subject matter in the process.

To be included in this collection, each activity had to meet the following criteria:

1. **It has a purpose in terms of educational goals.** This purpose must be clearly defined to children so they may gain the most benefit. An activity period should begin with a statement of purpose and end with a review of learnings. During the activity period itself, the emphasis should be on enjoyment of the learning experience.

2. **It can be carried out in an orderly way.** By "enjoyment" of the learning experience we do not mean to imply that children participate with unchecked enthusiasm. Children neither expect nor appreciate having their classroom turned into a boistrous playroom. After testing each activity, we omitted any which caused undue confusion or created excitement to the point where purpose was overshadowed.

3. **It is enjoyable for children.** If an activity is not enjoyable, it would not, of course, fulfill our goal of providing interesting incentive for learning.

While some of the activities included may appear on first glance to be absurdly simple, they are ones in which class after class of youngsters has participated with complete enjoyment.

4. **It does not require extensive teacher-preparation.** Often in an activity program much preparation of materials is required. This fact in itself makes some teachers shun activities completely because, "They're too much work." Or, at the other extreme, a very conscientious teacher may become so involved in preparing materials that she has little time for her own personal life.

Many have discovered the happy medium: letting children help. Children can do such tasks as cutting ruled tagboard into squares and lettering them to make their own sound cards. They can illustrate charts, or keep the storage place for activity materials neat and clean. In many of the activities in this text, specific suggestions are given as to how children may help in the necessary preparation. Far from being "busy work," these are constructive contributions which increase the opportunities for the group's learning experiences.

This book's illustrations, done by the author, are used purposely to show that the teacher's drawings on the board or charts need not be elaborate, nor even skillful, to put across the point intended.

The language arts activities suggested in this text have been used successfully in actual classrooms. Our list is by no means complete, but we hope it will suggest the **kinds** of activities that will make the language arts program more interesting and meaningful for your children. Just as you experiment with spices in your kitchen, we hope you will experiment with these activities in your classroom—adding a little here, taking away a little there—until you achieve just the right "flavor" to give your children a happy and purposeful learning experience.

SEATWORK ACTIVITIES
SECTION 1
PHONETIC ANALYSIS

1. PICTURE PUZZLES (Grades 2-6)

A. Preparation and Materials: Children will need drawing paper, pencils, and crayons.

Divide the blackboard into squares. In each square draw an object whose name contains the letter or letters for one of the sounds studied in the phonics class. Write in each square the name of the object pictured, omitting the letters which give the sounds being stressed in the lesson.

Example:

B. **Introduction to the Class:** Today I have a new kind of puzzle for you. To do this puzzle, you will first need to fold your paper into thirds each way.

Now draw the picture in the first square. Say the word to yourself. Listen to the way it begins. The word under each picture is complete except for the letter for the first sound. Decide what that first sound should be, and use the letter that says the sound to complete the word. Then go on and do the other squares in the same way.

C. **Variation:** To adapt this activity for use as a group game, draw a similar diagram on the board.

Call on one child at a time to fill in the missing letters. As a child fills in the letter, he should say aloud first the name of the object, then the missing sound, and last the letter (or letters) which makes that sound.

2. HIDE THE LETTERS (Grades 2-3)

A. Preparation and Materials: Children will need drawing paper, pencils, and crayons.

Draw any scene on the board, or ask the children to draw whatever scene they would enjoy making.

B. Introduction to the Class: I have drawn a picture on the board. I would like you to use your crayons and draw the same picture. Then look at each object in the picture. Say its name to yourself. Listen to the way it begins. Decide what the first letter of that word would be. Write that first letter on top of the object you have drawn.

Then look at another object and do the same thing. See how many objects you can label with the letters that say their correct beginning sounds.

Example:

C. Variations: 1. Ask children to draw a scene

begin with "s," for example. This, of course, would give more stress to that particular sound.

2. To adapt this activity for use as a group game, draw a scene on the board and call on one child at a time to label each object with its initial consonant. Ask him to say aloud the name of the object, the beginning sound, and the letter which makes that sound as he writes.

3. LONG VOWELS (Grades 2-6)

A. Preparation and Materials: Children will need writing paper, pencils, and crayons.

Draw five pictures at the top of the board, each one containing a different long-vowel sound.

Divide the lower part of the board into three sections. Use these sections to list words containing long-vowel sounds. After each word, draw a short blank line.

Example:

1.	2.	3. 4. 5.

cute 5	time __	meat __
feet 2	use __	line __
name 1	bone __	gave __
tone __	cake __	hope __

B. Introduction to the Class: At the top of the

board, you see five pictures. The name of each picture contains a long-vowel sound. Let's say the name of each picture together, and listen for each long-vowel sound.

Now you may fold your paper in thirds. At the top, you may draw and number the five pictures, just as I have done on the board. Under these, you may use the three columns to list the words you see on the board.

The first word is "cute." Which long-vowel sound do you hear in "cute," Dick? Yes, the long "u." Which picture at the top of the page has the same sound? Yes, number 5, "music." Can you hear the long "u" in both "cute" and "music"? So I will write "5" on the line after "cute" to show that this word and the word for the fifth picture both have the same vowel sound. (The teacher demonstrates.)

Do the other words in the same way. Say the word to yourself. Find the picture at the top of the page which has the same vowel sound. Put the number of that picture by the word.

C. Variation: Illustrate the five short vowels at the top of the page, and list words containing short-vowel sounds. Children work in the same manner, matching each word with the picture that has the same short-vowel sound.

4. DETECTIVE (Grades 2-3)

A. Preparation and Materials: Children will need writing paper and pencils.

Write several sentences on the board.

Example:

---

1. Are you going to the store today? _____12_____

2. The snow is very beautiful. _____10_____

3. Jane likes to help Mother. _____

4. I can see red and yellow flowers. _____

5. Today is Wednesday. _____

6. Father is raking the yard. _____

B. Introduction to the Class: Today I would like to see if you are good detectives. We have studied which letters are vowels, and I would like to see how well you can find them in the sentences I have written on the board.

Write one sentence at a time. Then look at each word in that sentence and count the number of vowels you see. Write that number at the end of the sentence. Don't forget that "y" is counted as a vowel if there is no other vowel in the same syllable.

C. Variations: Children can be "detectives" and find almost any sounds you wish to train them to notice. For example, they might find little words hiding in bigger words ("at" in "cat," etc.) find double consonants, long-vowel sounds, root words with endings, etc.

5. PICTURE STORIES (Grades 1-3)

A. Preparation and Materials: Children will need writing paper, pencils, and crayons.

Write several sentences on the board. Omit some

of the initial consonants and put a picture "clue" above these words.

Example:

1. The boy and girl read books.
2. My _og likes _ones.
3. The _ig lives in the _arn.
4. Jack has a _agon, _all, and _orn.

B. Introduction to the Class: I have written several sentences on the board, but I have left out the beginning letters of some of the words. The short line will tell you where a letter is missing. There is a picture "clue" above each of these words to help you know what the complete word should be.

Copy one sentence at a time. When you come to a missing letter, look at the picture above that word. Say its name to yourself. Listen to the way it begins. Decide what letter would say that sound. Then write that letter on the blank line to complete the word.

You may draw the picture "clues" above these words if you wish.

6. RECOGNIZING LONG VOWEL SOUNDS (Grades 1-3)

A. Preparation and Materials: Children will need drawing paper, pencils, and crayons.

Divide the blackboard into squares. In each square, illustrate an object containing a long-vowel sound. Draw a short blank line in the lower right-hand corner of each square.

Explain to children that the word illustrated in the third square of row 3 is "music." Words capable of illustration and which contain a long "u" sound are not common, and most must be explained to children in order to get the desired response.

Example:

B. Introduction to the Class: Today I would like to see how well you can hear long-vowel sounds. First I would like you to fold your drawing paper into thirds each way. In the first square, draw the picture you see on the board. It is a cane. Which long-vowel sound do you hear in the word "cane," Jane? Yes, long "a." So you will write "a" on the blank line at the bottom of that square. Then go on and do the other squares in the same way.

C. Variation: Illustrate words containing short-vowel sounds in each square. Ask children to draw the pictures and write the short-vowel sounds they hear.

7. DISTINGUISHING BETWEEN LONG AND SHORT VOWEL SOUNDS (Grades 2-6)

A. Preparation and Materials: Children will need drawing paper, pencils, and crayons.

Divide the board into squares. In each square illustrate a word which contains either the long or short sound of the same vowel. Label each picture.

Example: long and short "i"

B. Introduction to the Class: In each square of the board I have drawn an object which contains either the long or short sound of "i." Each picture is labeled.

You will need to fold your drawing paper in thirds each way. Next draw the picture and write the word in the first square. Then say the name of that word to yourself. If you hear a short "i," write "short" in that square. If you hear a long "i," write "long."

The first picture shows a pin. Do you hear a short or a long "i" in **pin,** Bobby? Yes, short. So you would write "short" in that square. Do the other squares in the same way.

8. SOUND PICTURES (Grades 1-2)

Divide the board into squares. In each square, write a different letter (or letters) which says a sound already studied by the class.

Example:

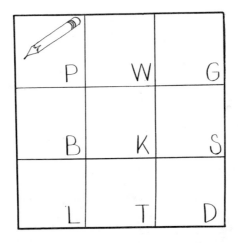

B. Introduction to the Class: First fold your drawing paper into thirds each way. Now look at the first square on the board. The letter 'p" is written in it. Can you think of a word that begins with a "p" sound, Delores? **Pencil, pig, pail, purse.** Yes, those are correct. You may draw in that square anything you can think of, the name of which starts with "p." Then go on to the next square. Say the sound to yourself and then draw in the square a picture of something that begins with that sound.

C. Variation: To adapt this activity for use as a group game, draw a similar diagram on the board and call on one child at a time to illustrate an object beginning with each of the given sounds. Before he draws, he should say aloud, first, the name of the letter, then the sound it makes, and last, the name of the object which he has chosen to draw and which begins with that letter and sound.

9. MARKING VOWELS (Grades 2-8)

A. Preparation and Materials: Children will need writing paper and pencils.

Make a list of words on the board. Some should contain short-vowel sounds, some long-vowel sounds, and some silent vowels.

Example:

1. hŏt	7. fish	13. hole
2. bōat	8. cap	14. bed
3. chĭldrĕn	9. invite	15. rain
4. tīme	10. which	16. music
5. get	11. cut	17. read
6. leave	12. use	18. he

B. Introduction to the Class: First, I would like you to fold your paper in thirds to make three columns. Next, you may write the list of words that you see on the board.

Now say the first word, **hot,** to yourself. The vowel in that word is "o." Is the "o" short or long, Jerry? Yes, short, so put the mark for a short vowel above the "o" like this (teacher demonstrates).

Will you tell me how the vowels sound in the second word, **boat,** Karen? Yes, the "o" is long

- 16 -

(teacher marks the "o" long) and the "a" is silent (teacher crosses out the silent "a").

You may mark the vowels in the other words in the same way. Show whether each vowel is short, long, or silent.

10. SYLLABLES (Grades 2-8)

A. Preparation and Materials: Children will need writing paper and pencils.

Make a list of words on the board.

Example:

1. grandmother *grand-moth-er*	7. table
2. understand *un-der-stand*	8. elephant
3. happy *hap-py*	9. ribbon
4. going	10. queen
5. look	11. prettiest
6. window	12. after

B. Introduction to the Class: Will you please fold your paper in half to make two columns? Now copy the list of words you see on the board.

We are going to divide these words into syllables. Remember the rule for dividing words, "There are as many divisions in a word as there are vowel sounds in the word."* How many syllables are there in the first word, **grandmother**, Jack? Yes, three. How would you divide that word into three syllables? Yes, **grand-moth-er** (teacher writes the divided word on the board).

---

*Note: This is quoted from STEPS TO MASTERY OF WORDS, Teachers Guide Book ***, Nadine Fillmore, author, and published by Educational Service, Inc., Benton Harbor, Michigan, price $1.50. The author has found this book very helpful.

You may divide the other words in the same way. First, say the word to yourself. Think how many syllables there will be. Then, divide the word and write it just as we have done this first one together.

11. SOUNDING OUT NEW WORDS (Grades 2-8)

A. Preparation and Materials: Children will need drawing paper, pencils, and crayons.

Divide the blackboard into squares. In each square, illustrate an object whose name is spelled completely phonetically.

Example:

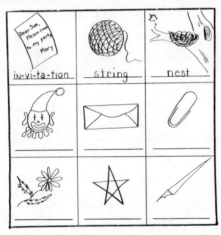

B. Introduction to the Class: Will you please fold your drawing paper in thirds each way to make squares just as you see on the board?

In each square, is a picture. I would like you to draw that picture, and then say its name to yourself. Each of these words is spelled just as it sounds. I would like to see how well you can sound out those words and write them by syllables under each picture.

12. ILLUSTRATING "MAGICAL E"* (Grades 3-6)

A. Preparation and Materials: Children will need drawing paper, pencils, and crayons.

Divide the board into four squares. In each square, write two sentences, one containing a "magical e" word, and the other containing the same word minus the final "e."

Divide the top of each square into two parts. Number these sections "1" and "2."

Underline the stressed word in each sentence.

Example:

1. It is _past_ 12 o'clock.
2. I will _paste_ a picture.

1. I _can_ jump very high.
2. The old man has a _cane._

1. Sue will _pin_ up her picture.
2. See the _pine_ trees.

1. Mary has a _rip_ in her dress.
2. The apples are _ripe._

B. Introduction to the Class: First I would like you to fold your paper in fourths to make four sections just as you see on the board.

Will you read the sentences you see in the first square, Dick? What do you notice about the words underlined in these two sentences, Yvonne? Yes, they are alike except one has the "magical e" added. Let's read together the underlined words in each of the four squares, and listen to how the word changes when the "magical e" is added.

*See Appendix for explanation of "Magical E."

I would like you to write the two sentences you see at the bottom of each square. As you write them, listen to the change in the underlined word when "e" is added.

Then divide the space at the top of each square into two parts. Number them "1" and "2." In the first space draw a picture to illustrate the first sentence. In the second space draw a picture to tell about the second sentence.

Then do the other squares the same way.

13. STORY PUZZLES (Grades 2-8)

A. Preparation and Materials: Children will need writing paper and pencils.

Have the children help compose a short creative story, which you write on the board as they dictate. After the story is complete, ask several children to read the story aloud to the class.

Then go through the story and erase parts of words; blend letters, initial consonants, endings, digraphs, etc. Put a line to show where the missing letters should go.

B. Introduction to the Class: Now that I have erased parts of the story, I would like to have Jerry try to read it. Please "think out loud" the sounds of the missing letters as you read, Jerry.

Would you do the same please, Karen? (Continue in this manner until you are sure the children know how to fill in the missing letters.)

Now I would like to have each of you write this story. Whenever you come to a blank line, fill in the missing letters as you write.

14. SAILING (Grades 2-3)

A. Preparation and Materials: Mimeograph sheets showing the illustration given below. Give one of these sheets to each child in the class. Children will need pencils and crayons.

Example:

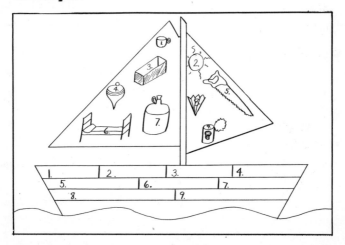

B. Introduction to the Class: On the sails of this boat, you will find many pictures. Each picture has a number on it. What picture has the number 1 on it, Mary? Yes, the cup. How do you spell **cup,** David? Yes, **c-u-p.**

Now can you find the number "1" on the bottom of the boat? Will you write the word **cup** in the space after that number? Then find picture "2." Write that word in the space by number "2" on the bottom of the boat. You may do the others in the same way.

After you have finished writing all the words, you may color the pictures.

C. Variation: To adapt this activity for use as a group game, draw a similar diagram on the board.

Call on one child at a time to write in the proper places the correct spelling for each of the pictured objects.

15. COLOR THE CIRCLE (Grade 1)

A. Preparation and Materials: Mimeograph sheets showing the illustration below. Give one of these sheets to each child in the classroom. Each child will need crayons.

Example:

B. Introduction to the Class: What letter do you see written in the middle of the circle, Jane? Yes, "d." What sound does that letter make, Mike? Yes, "d."

I would like you to look at each picture around the circle. Say the name of each picture to yourself. If that picture begins with a "d" sound, color it. If it does **not** begin with a "d" sound, **do not** color it.

16. CIRCLE WORDS (Grades 1-2)

A. Preparation and Materials: Mimeograph sheets similar to that shown in the example below.

Give one of these sheets to each child in the class. Children will need pencils and crayons.

Example:

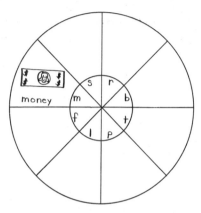

B. Introduction to the Class: In each space in the outside circle, I would like you to write a word which begins with the letter you see in the inner circle. After you have written all the words, you may put a picture in each section to show the word you have written.

C. Variation: To adapt this activity for use as a group game, draw a similar diagram on the board. Call on one child at a time to draw an object which begins with each of the given sounds. Before he draws, he should say aloud, first the letter, then the sound it makes, and last the name of the object which he has chosen to draw and which begins with this sound.

17. MATCH THE TWINS (Grade 1)

A. Divide the board into sections. In each section, write one column of words, and another showing the initial consonants of these words. Children will need writing paper and pencils.

Example:

jam	c	wagon	d
gun	f	yellow	h
nut	j	vase	s
cake	b	sun	w
fox	m	doll	p
bib	n	puppy	y
mother	g	hat	v

B. Introduction to the Class: First, I would like you to fold your writing paper in half to make two sections, just as you see on the board. Write the words and letters in each section, just as you see them on the board.

Next, I would like you to draw a line from each word to the letter in the second column which tells how that word begins.

The first word is **jam.** How does that word begin, Alice? Yes, with "j," so I will draw a line from **jam** to the letter "j." (Teacher demonstrates on the board.)

You may match the other words and beginning letters in the same way.

18. INDIAN CHIEF (Grade 1)

A. Preparation and Materials: Mimeograph pictures of an Indian headdress. On each feather, write a word, having the majority of words beginning with the letter in the feather pictured in the lower right-hand corner of the sheet.

Children will need crayons.

Example:

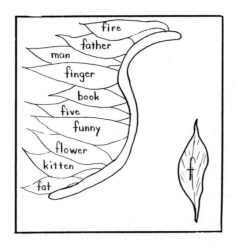

B. Introduction to the Class: Would you like to be an Indian Chief? You may be one if you can color the feathers in this headdress in exactly the right way.

Look at the feather at the bottom of the page. What letter is written on that feather, John? Yes, "f." Now look at the feathers in the Indian's headdress. You may color only the feathers on which is written a word beginning with "f."

19. MAKING NEW WORDS (Grades 2-8)

A. Preparation and Materials: List on the board three columns of letters whose sounds have been studied by the class. For drill in foundation letter combinations, the list might be:

r an	—ap	—at
p en	—ep	—et
—in	—ip	—it
—on	—op	—ot
—un	—up	—ut

Children will need writing paper and pencils.

B. Introduction to the Class: First, please fold your writing paper into thirds to make three columns as you see on the board.

Now write the letters for the first sound. What is that sound, Doris? Yes, "an." Can you think of a word that contains "an," Billy? Yes, **ran.**

What letter would you need to put in front of "an" to make **ran,** Susan? Yes, "r." (Teacher writes "r" in front of "an" on the board.)

I would like you to write the letters for each of these sounds on your paper. Say the sound to yourself. Think of a word which contains that sound. Then add whatever letters you would need to write the complete word.

C. Variation: To adapt this activity for use as a group game, divide the class into two teams. Designate a blackboard area for each team to use. In each section, list a group of sounds as shown in the example above. You may give each team the same sound list or different lists.

The first child from each team will go to the board and complete **any** word. He then gives the chalk to the next child on his team who will complete another word, and so on.

The team which first correctly completes every word on its list is the winner.

SEATWORK ACTIVITIES
SECTION 2
STRUCTURAL ANALYSIS

1. RHYMING WORDS PUZZLE (Grades 1-2)

A. Preparation and Materials: Divide the blackboard into squares. In each square, illustrate two rhyming words. Label one picture in each square. Children will need drawing paper, pencils, and crayons.

Example:

B. Introduction to the Class: Today, we are going to do a rhyming puzzle. First, you will need to take your drawing paper and fold it in thirds each way. You may put your crayons and pencils at the top of your desk.

On the board, you will see two pictures in each square. You may use your crayons to draw these same pictures in each square of your paper.

Let's look at the first square. It shows a bear and a pear. Can you hear the two words rhyme? If **bear** is spelled b-e-a-r, how do you think **pear** would be spelled, Steven? That's right, p-e-a-r. All you had to do was change the first letter, because the last part of each word sounds alike, and is spelled alike.

First, draw the pictures in each square of your paper. Then use your pencil to write the name of the first object. Then you will need to think how that word could be changed to say the name of the second object. Write that name on your paper.

C. Variation: To use this same activity as a group game, put a similar diagram on the board. Call on one child at a time to fill in the missing words.

2. PICTURE PUZZLES (Grades 1-3)

A. Preparation and Materials: Divide the blackboard into squares. In each square, draw a picture. Write three similarly structured words by each picture, one of which is the correct name for the picture.

Children will need drawing paper, pencils, and crayons.

Example:

B. Introduction to the Class: To do our picture puzzle today, you will first need to fold your drawing paper in thirds each way. Now you may take out your pencils and crayons and put them at the top of your desks.

First you may use your crayons to draw in each square the pictures just as they are in the board. Notice there are three words by each picture. Use your pencils to write these words. One word is the correct name for the picture. The other two words look almost like it, so you will need to look and think carefully. Take your pencils and draw a ring around the word which correctly names each picture.

3. FIND IT (Grades 1-3)

A. Preparation and Materials: List several directions on the board for children to follow. Under each, list 4 words, some of which fit the given directions.

Children will need writing paper and pencils.

Example:

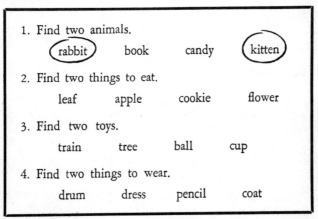

B. Introduction to the Class: Today I will see how well you can find things. On the board, are the directions which tell you what to find. Will you read the first direction, Sally? Yes, it says "Find two animals."

Below this are four words. Can you find two animal names among those words, Scott? You will need to look and think carefully. Will you come up to the board and draw a ring around the two animals you have found, Scott? Very good!

As you do this work at your seat, first read the directions you have copied on your paper. As you write the four words beneath it, look carefully at each word. Draw a ring around the two words which the directions asked you to find.

4. INITIAL CONSONANTS (Grades 1-3)

A. Preparation and Materials: Children will need writing paper, crayons, and pencils.

Write sentences on the board, and in each sentence give children two choices for one word to complete that sentence. Make the two choices alike except for their initial consonants. Draw a picture "clue" for the appropriate word.

Example:

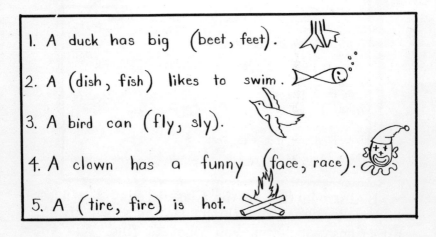

1. A duck has big (beet, feet).

2. A (dish, fish) likes to swim.

3. A bird can (fly, sly).

4. A clown has a funny (face, race).

5. A (tire, fire) is hot.

B. Introduction to the Class: On the board, are several sentences. Each sentence is complete except for the last word. You have two choices from which to pick the word which will correctly complete the sentence. The picture "clue" at the end of each sentence will help you know the meaning of the correct word.

Write one sentence at a time on your paper. Listen carefully to the sounds of the letters in the two words from which you may choose. Write just the one you think will correctly complete the sentence. You may draw the picture "clues" at the end of each sentence if you wish.

5. RHYMING WORDS (Grades 1-2)

A. Preparation and Materials: Each child will need writing paper and a pencil.

On the board, write a list of words, and beside it a list of rhyming words.

Example:

1. say	win	7. ran	cake
2. pin	paw	8. bump	took
3. hot	sing	9. make	bunny
4. saw	day	10. look	jump
5. ring	not	11. funny	so
6. hand	sand	12. no	man

B. Introduction to the Class: We have talked together about rhyming words, and we have found that words which rhyme often end with the same

- 33 -

letters. Today, we shall see how well you can find rhyming words.

First, fold your writing paper in half. In each half, write the two columns of words just as they are on the board. Then draw a line to match the words which rhyme.

C. Variation: Write a similar word list on the board and call on one child at a time to match rhyming words. This activity would be good as a quick review.

6. CONTRACTIONS (Grades 2-3)

A. Preparation and Materials: Children will need writing paper and pencils.

On the board, make a list of contractable words, and beside them a list of the contracted forms.

Example:

1. does not	won't	6. was not	don't
2. can not	couldn't	7. should not	wasn't
3. will not	can't	8. has not	hasn't
4. could not	haven't	9. do not	wouldn't
5. have not	doesn't	10. would not	shouldn't

B. Introduction to the Class: We have been studying word contractions, and today I would like to see how well you can remember what those contractions stand for.

First, please fold your writing paper in half. Next, write the two columns of words just as they are on the board. Then, draw a line to match the long form of each word to its contracted form.

C. Variation: Write a similar word list on the board and call on one child at a time to match contractions. This activity would serve as a quick group review lesson.

7. RHYMING WORDS (Grade 1-2)

A. Preparation and Materials: Children will need writing paper and pencils.

On the board, list a column of words, and beside each write several similarly structured words, some of which rhyme with the first word in that row.

Example:

1. ring	sing	rug	thing
2. moon	some	soon	spoon
3. dime	dine	time	lime
4. sat	rat	sit	bat
5. grape	drape	grab	shape
6. same	came	name	some

B. Introduction to the Class: For our work today, you will need to write one row of words at a time, just as they are on the board. Underline the first word in that row.

Then look carefully at that underlined word. See if you can find other words in the same row which rhyme with that first word. Circle the rhyming words you find.

8. HIDE AND SEEK (Grades 2-6)

A. Preparation and Materials: Children will need paper and pencils.

On the board, list words which contain smaller words within them.

Example:

mon(key)	torn	pin
(let)ter	rat	lamp
basket	visit	chant
father	chair	today
paper	string	pencil
stop	boats	fact

B. Introduction to the Class: Yesterday, we talked about the little words which are sometimes inside bigger words. Today, I would like to see how well you can find these little words.

First, you will need to fold your papers in thirds. Write one word at a time. Circle the little word you find hiding inside it. In some of these words, there are two or more little words hiding. When you find more than one little word hiding, circle each of the little words.

9. MAKING RHYMES (Grades 1-2)

A. Preparation and Materials: Children will need drawing paper, pencils, and crayons.

Divide the blackboard into squares. In each square, write a two-line rhyme omitting the last word of the second line. Illustrate each poem.

Example:

A pig
Is very _big_ .

A man who is tall
Can look over the ___ .

My dog thinks it's fun
To jump and ___ .

The clown
Is upside ___ .

B. Introduction to the Class: First, you will need to fold your drawing paper into halves each way. Now let's look at the first section of the board. There is a picture, and part of a poem about the picture.

The picture shows a pig. The poem says, "A pig is very _____." What word do you think I could write in that blank so the second line would rhyme with the first, Tommy? Yes, **big.** Then the rhyme would say, "The pig is very big." You can finish the other rhymes in the same way.

You will want to use your crayons for the pictures, but remember to use your pencils for all the writing.

10. CHANGING WORDS (Grades 2-3)

A. Preparation and Materials: Children will need writing paper and pencils.

On the board, make a list of words which can be easily changed to new words by changing the initial consonants.

Example:

---

1. play — *day, may, say, way; gay, hay*

2. sat

3. lump

4. came

5. sing

6. make

B. Introduction to the Class: I have listed 6 words on the board. Beside each word I would like you to write as many rhyming words as you can think of. Remember that rhyming words often end the same way but begin with different sounds. See how many ways you can change the beginning of each word to make new words which rhyme.

11. COMPOUND WORD PUZZLES (Grades 2-6)

A. Preparation and Materials: Children will need writing paper, pencils, and crayons.

On the board, illustrate pairs of words which can be put together to form compound words.

B. Introduction to the class: Here is a new kind of puzzle for you. If you will say the names of each of the two pictures in a row, you will hear a new compound word.

Draw one pair of pictures at a time. After these pictures, write the new compound word you hear. If you can spell each word separately, all you need to do is join them together to spell the new compound word. (See next page for example.)

Example:

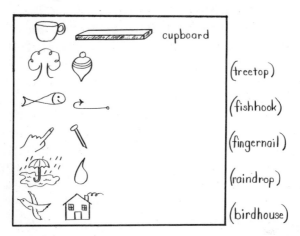

cupboard

(treetop)

(fishhook)

(fingernail)

(raindrop)

(birdhouse)

12. LIKENESSES AND DIFFERENCES IN WORDS (Grades 4-8)

A. Preparation and Materials: Children will need writing paper and pencils.

List pairs of similarly structured words on the board.

Example:

1. going	looking	7. hit	hat
2. today	tonight	8. forget	forward
3. book	foot	9. barn	farm
4. get	got	10. start	card
5. could	should	11. make	take
6. grow	grass	12. return	rewind

B. Introduction to the Class: On the board, I have listed pairs of words which look somewhat alike. First write one pair of words on your paper. Circle the parts in each word which are alike. Draw a line under the parts which are different.

Let's look at the first pair of words together. They are **going** and **looking**. Which parts of these words are exactly alike, Billy? Yes, each word ends with "ing." So I will circle the "ing" in each word. (Teacher demonstrates.)

What is different about these words, Susan? Yes, the first letters. So I will draw a line under the first letters of each word (teacher demonstrates).

You may do the others just as we did this pair of words together.

13. SUPERLATIVE ENDINGS (Grades 2-3)

A. Preparation and Materials: Children will need writing paper and pencils.

On the board, write such questions as **Which is tallest? Which is biggest?** etc. After each question, draw three various-sized objects.

Example:

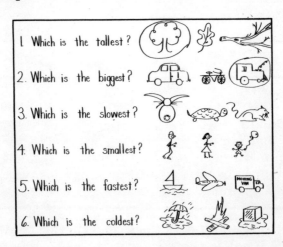

1. Which is the tallest?
2. Which is the biggest?
3. Which is the slowest?
4. Which is the smallest?
5. Which is the fastest?
6. Which is the coldest?

B. Introduction to the Class: We have been

studying the "est" ending, and today I will see how well you remember what that ending means. What does the first question ask, Roger? That's right, and which object is the tallest? Yes, the tree, so I will draw a circle around the tree (teacher demonstrates).

Write one sentence at a time on your paper. Draw the three objects after the sentence. Then circle the object that answers the question.

14. ROOT WORDS AND ENDINGS (Grades 2-6)

A. Preparation and Materials: Children will need paper and pencils.

List root words with endings on the board. Example:

1. <u>look</u>ed	6. opening	11. kittens
2. <u>work</u>er	7. jumped	12. walked
3. seeing	8. quickly	13. raining
4. runs	9. sooner	14. teacher
5. talking	10. faster	15. slowly

B. Introduction to the Class: Today, I would like to see how well you can find the root part of a word and the ending of a word. First, fold your paper in thirds. Then write one word at a time on your paper, using three columns as I have done on the board. Underline each root word and circle each ending.

Let's try the first one together. The word is **looked.** What is the root word, Mary? Yes, **look,** so I will draw a line under **look.** What is the ending,

- 41 -

David? Yes, "ed," so I will draw a ring around "ed." You may do the other words in the same way.

15. COMPARATIVE ENDINGS (Grades 2-3)

A. Preparation and Materials: Children will need writing paper, pencils, and crayons.

Divide the board into squares. In each square, write three comparative adjectives and illustrate each.

Example:

B. Introduction to the Class: We have been studying the endings, "er" and "est." Today, I would like to see how well you remember what these endings mean.

First, you will need to fold your paper in half both ways. Next, write the three words in each square, just as I have done on the board. Then you are ready to draw the illustrations. Remember, we are comparing things, so be very careful to make one picture small, one medium, and one large, just as they are shown on the board.

Next, draw a line from each word to the picture it describes.

16. VERB CONJUGATIONS (Grades 4-8)

A. Preparation and Materials: Children will need writing paper and pencils.

Divide the board into four columns. Label the first column **Root Words**, the second **Now**, the next **Yesterday**, and the last **Tomorrow**.

In the first column, list root words which are conjugated by adding the usual endings and/or helping words (not words which change their tense by a change within the word itself).

Example:

ROOT	NOW	YESTERDAY	TOMORROW
1. walk	he is walking	he walked	he will walk
2. jump			
3. work			
4. talk			
5. look			
6. spell			

B. Introduction to the Class: We have been talking about how words change by adding new endings or helping words to show whether something is happening now, happened yesterday, or will happen tomorrow. I would like to see how well you remember those endings and helping words.

First, fold your paper into four columns, and label each column as I have done on the board. Next, write one root word in the column where it belongs.

The first root word is **walk.** How would we write that if it were happening right now, Linda? Yes, "He is walking." So you may write that in the column labeled **Now.** (The teacher demonstrates.)

If it happened yesterday, how would we write it, class? Yes, "He walked." You may write "He walked," in the column labeled **Yesterday,** like this (The teacher demonstrates.)

And if it will happen tomorrow? Yes, "He will walk." You may write that in the last column. (The teacher demonstrates.)

Now you are ready to write the second root word and to think how it will change by adding new endings and helping words to show when the action occurred.

17. COMPOUND WORDS (Grades 2-3)

A. Preparation and Materials: Children will need writing paper and pencils.

List on the board columns of words which can be matched to form compound words.

Example:

1. grand	side	8. barn	cake
2. out	stairs	9. in	cup
3. snow	mother	10. tea	to
4. up	cloth	11. pan	night
5. table	bow	12. finger	yard
6. tea	man	13. to	ball
7. rain	pot	14. basket	nail

B. Introduction to the Class: I have written two columns of words on the board. Words in the first column can be matched with words in the second column to form compound words.

The first word is **grand.** Do you see a word in the second column which could be put with **grand** to form a compound word, Barbara? Yes, **mother.** What would the compound word be then, Barbara? Yes, **grandmother.** Would you please come up and draw a line from **grand** to **mother** to show that those two words can form a compound word?

You may write the two columns of words on your paper, and then match them just as we have done the first one together.

18. RECOGNIZING COMPLETE SENTENCES
(Grades 2-6)

A. Preparation and Materials: Children will need writing paper and pencils.

On the board, list groups of words, some of which are complete sentences. Put a blank line after each group of words.

Example:

1. One beautiful day_____no_____

2. Dick and Susan are good friends. __yes__

3. After school I went _____

4. Sally jumped over the _____

5. In school we learn to read. _____

6. Spring will soon be here. _____

B. Introduction to the Class: We have talked this week about complete sentences. Today, I would like to see if you can find some complete sentences.

On the board, are several groups of words. Some of the groups tell complete thoughts, and they are sentences. Those that do not tell complete thoughts are not sentences.

Write each group of words on your paper. If it is a sentence, write "yes" on the blank after it. If it is not a sentence, write "no."

(In higher grades children may be asked to add words to express complete thoughts.)

19. PUNCTUATION AND CAPITALIZATION
(Grades 2-8)

A. Preparation and Materials: Children will need writing paper and pencils.

Write several groups of words on the board. Use no capital letters and no punctuation. Vary the difficulty of the vocabulary and sentence structure to fit the level of your group.

Example:

1. dick and susan like to play together
2. will you give that to me
3. don found new york on the map
4. mother and i will go away
5. do you like that book
6. shall i ask bill and tom to come

B. Introduction to the Class: Tom, would you please read the first group of words you see on the board? What did you notice that was strange about this group of words, Tom? Yes, it has no capital letters and no punctuation. Where would you use capital letters or punctuation marks in this sentence, Alice? (Teacher should help children to see where capital letters and punctuation marks should be added.)

Now I would like you to copy each of these groups of words and use capital letters and punctuation marks wherever they are needed.

C. Variations: Write the material on the board in paragraph form, and make errors in capitalization, punctuation, spelling, and general sentence structure.

Children should then be asked to re-write the paragraph, correcting as many errors as they can find.

Sample Paragraph:

I offen play base ball with my frieds after shool when we fanish play base ball we sometime have a cool drink and when we go home.

Same Paragraph Corrected:

I often play baseball with my friends after school. When we finish playing baseball, we sometimes have a cool drink and then we go home.

SEATWORK ACTIVITIES
SECTION 3
READING FOR MEANING

1. YES OR NO? (Grades 1-3)

A. Preparation and Materials: Children will need writing paper and pencils.

Write several sentences on the board, some being true statements while others are false.

Example:

---

1. A dog can fly. _____**No**_____

2. A baby is very little. ____**Yes**____

3. Birds like to sing. _____

4. Cookies grow on trees. _____

5. Elephants have big ears. _____

6. Snow falls in the winter. _____

B. Introduction to the Class: I have written some sentences on the board, which I would like you to copy. A blank line is after each sentence. Read each sentence to yourself. If what it says is true, write "yes" on the line after that sentence. If what it says is **not** true, write "no" after it. (This activity can be adapted to higher grade usage by using complex vocabulary and sentence structure.)

2. SCRAMBLED EGGS (Grades 2-4)

A. Preparation and Materials: Children will need writing paper and pencils.

On the board, write several sentences in which the words have been scrambled. Underline the word which will come first when the sentence is arranged in its proper order.

Example:

---

1. to <u>Jane</u> Mother store for went the.

2. likes play <u>Jack</u> to ball.

3. doll has <u>Susan</u> new a.

4. after cat mouse the ran <u>The</u>.

5. sunny <u>Today</u> day a is.

6. yard rake will the <u>Father</u>.

B. Introduction to the Class: How many of you have eaten scrambled eggs? They are eggs all mixed up together, aren't they? Today I have some scrambled sentences. The words are all mixed up just like scrambled eggs.

I would like to see if you can straighten out these words to make complete sentences. Let's look at the first one together. Will you read the words to yourself, please?

The word **Jane** is underlined. That means the word **Jane** will come first when we unscramble the words. Can you tell us how that sentence should read, Bill? Yes, "Jane went to the store for Mother." So you may write that on your paper.

Then do the other groups in the same way. Begin with the underlined word, and write the unscrambled sentence on your paper.

3. RIDDLES (Grades 1-2)

A. Preparation and Materials: Write four riddles on the board, omitting the words which tell the answers. Leave spaces above the riddles in which the children may illustrate their answers.

Children will need drawing paper, pencils, and crayons.

Example: (Hallowe'en theme)

Front   Back

I am orange.	I ride in the sky	I am black.	I am white.
I have a face.	on a broomstick.	I have four feet.	I say, "Boo!"
I make good pie.	I have a tall hat.	I say, "Mew."	I scare people.
I am a _____.	I am a _____.	I am a _____.	I am a _____.

B. Introduction to the Class: Will you please fold your drawing paper in half? Now you have two sections on the front, and two on the back.

In each section, I would like you to write the riddle you see on the board. As you write, think what the answer to that riddle might be. Write your answer on the blank in the last line. Then you may illustrate each riddle in the space at the top of each section.

4. PREPOSITIONAL PHRASES (Grades 1-2)

A. Preparation and Materials: Children will need drawing paper, pencils, and crayons.

Divide the blackboard into squares. In each square, write three prepositional phrases. Draw a picture in each square which correctly illustrates one of the prepositional phrases written there.

Example:

in a tree / on a tree / (under a tree)	by a wagon / (in a wagon) / over a wagon	under a chair / by a chair / on a chair
on a house / over a house / under a house	by a dish / in a dish / on a dish	over an arm / by an arm / on an arm
in a bowl / on a bowl / by a bowl	over a tree / on a tree / under a tree	by a table / over a table / on a table

B. Introduction to the Class: For our work today you will first need to fold your drawing paper in thirds each way. This will make nine sections.

On the board, you will see a picture and three phrases in each square. I would like you to draw those pictures and write those phrases on your paper.

In the first square, you see a tree with an apple under it. What do the three phrases say, Tommy? Very good! And which phrase best tells about the picture? Yes, "under the tree," because the apple is under the tree. So I will draw a ring around that phrase because it best tells about the picture.

Will you do the other squares in the same way? First, draw the picture and write the phrases. Then decide which phrase best tells about the picture. Draw a ring around that phrase.

5. ILLUSTRATING SENTENCES (Grades 1-3)

A. Preparation and Materials: Children will need drawing paper, pencils, and crayons.

Divide the board into squares. In each square, write a sentence which is capable of illustration.

Example:

Father is working in the yard.	Four boys are playing football.
These children are having a party.	The teacher is doing her work.

B. Introduction to the Class: Today, I would like to see how well you can read. I have written 4 sentences on the board. I would like you to fold your paper in four squares, and write one sentence in each square, just as it is on the board.

Then read each sentence carefully. Draw in each square exactly what the sentence tells you.

6. RIDDLES (Grades 1-3)

A. Preparation and Materials: Children will need writing paper, pencils, and crayons.

Draw five pictures at the top of the board. Number these pictures from 1 to 5. Under these, write five sentences, one sentence to describe each picture.

Example:

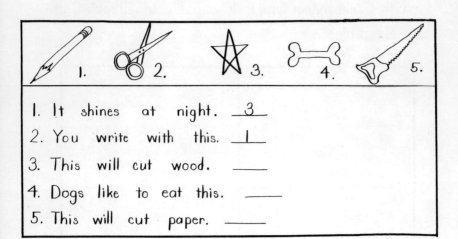

1. It shines at night. __3__
2. You write with this. __1__
3. This will cut wood. _____
4. Dogs like to eat this. _____
5. This will cut paper. _____

B. Introduction to the Class: To do this work you will first need to draw at the top of your paper the five pictures you see on the board. Number the pictures just as they are on the board.

Then write the first sentence. Read the sentence to yourself. It tells about one of the pictures. Find that picture. Write that number on the line after the sentence which describes it.

7. SELECTING WORDS (Grades 1-8)

A. Preparation and Materials: Children will need writing paper and pencils.

Write several sentences on the board. Omit one word from each sentence. List the missing words at the bottom of the board.

Example:

---

1. Dick's cat has _____**three**_____ kittens.

2. The house is over _____**there**_____.

3. The boys climbed a _____.

4. _____ is your coat?

5. Susan will be _____ soon.

  tree   there   here   three   where

B. Introduction to the Class: There is a word missing in each of the sentences on the board. The missing words are listed at the bottom. I would like you to write these sentences and fill in the words to complete the sentences.

8. READING TO GAIN INFORMATION
(Grades 2-8)

A. Preparation and Materials: Children will need writing paper and pencils.

Write a short story in one section of the blackboard. In another section, write questions about that story. Vary the vocabulary and plot complexity to fit the level of your group.

Sample Story:

Bill wanted to go to Jack's house to play. He asked Mother if he could go. Mother said he could not go because his work was not done.

Bill did his work. Then Mother said he could go and play with Jack.

Bill went to Jack's house. The boys played ball. They had a very good time.

Sample Questions:
1. Where did Bill want to go?
2. What did Mother say?
3. What did Bill do then?
4. Then what did Mother say?
5. What game did the boys play?
6. Did they have fun playing together?

B. Introduction to the Class: There is a story written on one section of the board. Some questions about the story are in another section. First read the story to yourself. Then read one question at a time. Think what the answer to that question would be. Write that answer on your paper. Make sure you answer each question **in a complete sentence.**

Remember, you do not copy the story. You do not copy the questions. All you need to write are the answers to the questions.

9. PERSON, PLACE, OR THING (Grades 2-3)

A. Preparation and Materials: Children will need writing paper and pencils.

Divide the board into 2 columns. Use these columns to list proper and common nouns.

Example:

1. Alice — person	7. Father
2. doll — thing	8. home
3. Detroit — place	9. pencil
4. apple	10. dime
5. Mrs. Brown	11. John
6. school	12. Michigan

B. Introduction to the Class: Each word listed

on the board is the name of a person, place, or a thing. I would like you to fold your paper in half to make two columns. In each column, list the words you see on the board. After each word write "person" if it is the name of a person, "place" if it is the name of a place, and "thing" if it is the name of a thing.

The first word is **Alice.** What would you write after that word, Mary? Yes, "person," because Alice is the name of a person. You may do the others in the same way.

10. SELECTING WORDS (Grades 2-8)

A. Preparation and Materials: Children will need writing paper and pencils.

Write several sentences on the board. Omit one word from each sentence. After each sentence, write three similarly structured words, one of which will correctly complete the sentence. Vary the difficulty of the vocabulary to meet the level of your group.

Example:

---

1. Father will **rake** the yard. (make   rake   take)
2. A **pig** is a farm animal. (big   dig   pig)
3. The school _____ is ringing. (doll   ball   bell)
4. Apples grow on a _____. (tree   there   three)
5. Mary _____ the pretty picture. (was   saw   sat)
6. It is _____ to play ball. (fan   fun   fin)

B. Introduction to the Class: You see six sentences written on the board. There is one word left out of each sentence. The missing word is one of the three written at the end of the sentence.

Will you read the first sentence to yourself, Sally? Try to find the word at the end of the sentence which belongs in the blank.

What word did you choose, Sally? Good, "rake." How would the complete sentence read then, Sally? Yes, "Father will **rake** the yard."

You will do the others in the same way. First read the sentences to yourself. Decide which of the three words at the end would best complete the sentence. Then write the sentence, putting in the missing word where you see the blank.

11. MATCHING (Grade 1)

A. Preparation and Materials: Children will need writing paper, pencils, and crayons.

Divide the board into four squares. In each square, write three phrases and illustrate one of these phrases.

Example:

a duck a cow a pig	a rake a shovel a hoe
a pen a pan a pin	a kitten a horse a rabbit

B. Introduction to the Class: First I would like

you to fold your writing paper into halves each way. You will then have four sections, just as I have on the board.

Write the three phrases in each square and draw the picture you see on the board. Then draw a line from the picture to the phrase which best describes it.

What picture do you see in the first square, Paul? Yes, a pig. Will you read the three phrases for us, David? Which phrase do you think best describes the picture, Cindy? Yes, **a pig**. So I will draw a line from the picture of the pig to the phrase that says **a pig** (teacher demonstrates on board).

You may do the other squares in the same way.

12. CATEGORIES (Grades 2-8)

A. Preparation and Materials: Children will need writing paper and pencils.

Example:

Food	Toys	Clothing
top	mittens	meat
shoe	milk	hat
cookie	doll	kite
wagon	candy	socks
apple	ball	train
coat	dress	jam

Divide the board into three sections. At the top of each section, write a major category, such as **food, toys, clothing**. Below these, list six words in each column, six being the names of food, six being the names of toys, and six being articles of clothing. List the words in no special order, putting some words from all three categories in each column.

For higher grades, use categories which require a higher degree of discrimination and a more difficult vocabulary.

B. Introduction to the Class: Will you please fold your paper into thirds to make three columns, just as you see on the board.

I would like you to write at the top of the columns the titles you see on the board. They are **food, toys,** and **clothing.**

I have written some other words on the board, but I have put them in no special order. I would like you to separate these words on your paper so that only the names of foods will be written in the **foods** column, only toys in the **toys** column, and only articles of clothing in the **clothing** column.

Be sure you have written the title of each column on your paper. Then read the first word listed below the titles. Decide whether that word names a food, toy, or article of clothing. Write that word in the proper column. Then read the next word, and write it where it belongs, and so on, until you have put all the words in their proper places.

13. TOY STORE PROBLEMS (Grades 2-3)

A. Preparation and Materials: Children will need writing paper, pencils, and crayons.

Draw five toys at the top of the board, and under each toy write its price. Under these, write several questions about the toys in the "store" which the children may answer either by filling a numerical answer in a blank or putting "yes" or "no" at the end of the sentence.

Example:

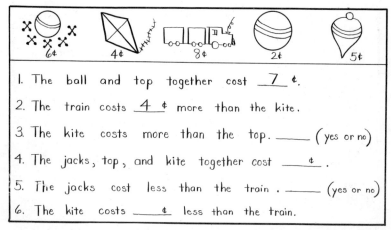

1. The ball and top together cost __7__ ¢.

2. The train costs __4__ ¢ more than the kite.

3. The kite costs more than the top. _____ (yes or no)

4. The jacks, top, and kite together cost _____ ¢ .

5. The jacks cost less than the train . _____ (yes or no)

6. The kite costs _____ ¢ less than the train.

B. Introduction to the Class: Today we are going to visit a toy store. In this store, you will find the toys I have drawn at the top of the board. You may color these toys at the top of your paper, and under each write its price, just as you see on the board.

Under the pictures, you will see several questions about the store. Some of the questions can be answered by filling in a price in the blank line. Some can be answered by writing "yes" or "no" at the end of the sentence.

Read each question carefully. Decide how that question could best be answered. Write your answer to each question.

14. MAKING A PICTURE (Grades 1-3)

A. Preparation and Materials: Write a short description of a picture on the board (see example). Children will need drawing paper and crayons.

Example:

Many children are playing outdoors at recess time. Two of the girls are jumping rope. Three of the boys are playing marbles.

The teacher is looking out the schoolroom window. Five trees are by the school.

The sun is shining. One small cloud is in the sky. Four birds are flying overhead.

B. Introduction to the Class: Today I would like you to read the story on the board and draw a picture showing exactly what the story tells you.

You may add extra things to your picture if you wish, but read the story carefully, and be sure to include everything it tells you.

15. WORDS THAT GO TOGETHER (Grades 2-6)

A. Preparation and Materials: Children will need writing paper and pencils.

List groups of four words on the blackboard, three of which are alike in some way.

Example:

1. apple	orange	carrot	pear
2. day	star	year	month
3. car	bus	train	house
4. cup	fork	knife	spoon
5. stove	hammer	saw	axe
6. river	ocean	mountain	lake

B. Introduction to the Class: I have written on the board several groups of words. Three words in each group are alike in some way, but one is different.

- 64 -

Write these groups of words on your paper. Find the three words in each group that are alike, and circle them.

16. MAP FUN (Grades 3-8)

A. Preparation and Materials: Children will need drawing paper, crayons, and pencils.

Draw on the blackboard a map similar to that shown below. Under it, list the directions, adapting the vocabulary to your particular grade level.

Example:

Directions:

1. There is a store on the S. E. corner of Pine Street. Write the word **store** on this corner.

2. There is a school on Oak Street. It is located near the N. W. corner. Draw a circle to represent the school, and write the word **school** under the circle.

3. A theater is across the street from the school. Draw two small squares to represent the theater.

4. Jack lives on Pine Street close to the S. W.

- 65 -

corner. Draw this symbol (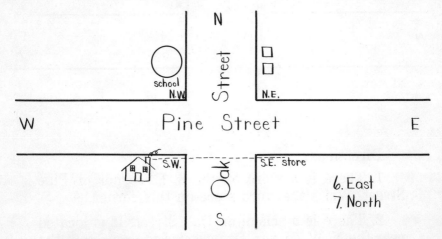) to represent his house.

5. Jack goes to the store for his Mother. Draw a broken line (------) to show the way he goes from his house to the store.

6. Is the theater east or west of the school?

7. Is the school north or south of Jack's house?

B. Introduction to the Class: I would like you to draw the map you see on the board. There are directions under the map for adding things to the map. Add those things the directions tell you.

Numbers 6 and 7 are questions. Write the answers to the questions in the lower right-hand corner of your paper.

(Child's finished paper should look like this:)

C. Variation

1. **Preparation and Materials:** Children will need writing paper and pencils.

Draw on the blackboard a map similar to that shown below. Under it list the given questions.

Example:

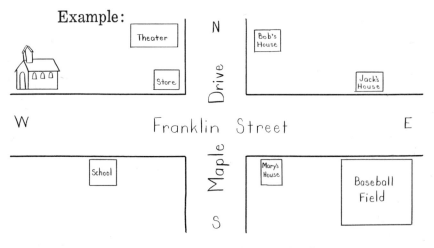

1. On which street does Mary live?

2. In which direction would Mary walk if she were going to walk to the theater?

3. Jack, Mary, and Bob walk to school together. Who lives nearest to the school? Who lives farthest from the school?

4. On which street is the church located?

5. Which is closer to the theater, the school or the store?

6. In which direction do the children walk when they first start home from school?

7. What is across the street from Jack's house?

8. Does Mary live north or south of Jack's house?

9. On which street is the school located?

10. On which street is the theater located?

2. Introduction to the Class: On the board, is a map. Under the map, are ten questions. Look at the map carefully. Then read each question carefully. Use your paper and pencil to answer each question

in a complete sentence. (Or, children may copy the questions and fill in short word answers.)

17. GRAPHS (Grades 3-5)

A. Preparation and Materials: Children will need writing paper and pencils.

Draw on the board a graph similar to that shown below. Under it, list the questions given.

Example:

Questions:

1. Who solved the least number of problems?
2. How many more problems were solved by Frank than Marie?
3. How many problems did Al solve?
4. Did Jane or Sue solve more problems?
5. Did Al solve more problems than Marie?
6. Who solved all the problems?
7. How many more problems were solved by Sue than by Al?
8. Marie solved how many fewer problems than Donald?
9. How many problems did Frank solve?
10. Who solved more problems, Bob or Sue?

B. Introduction to the Class: Here is a graph that tells a story about an arithmetic test. The numbers across the top are the numbers of the problems. The names at the left are the names of the children who took the test.

Study the graph first. See how many problems each student was able to work correctly. After you are sure of the graph, answer the questions below the graph. Write each answer **in a complete sentence.** (Or, children could copy the questions and write in short answers.)

18. FOLLOWING WRITTEN DIRECTIONS (Grades 4-8)

A. Preparation and Materials: Children will need drawing paper and pencils.

Draw on the blackboard the letters in the positions shown below. Under this, list the directions given.

Example:

Directions:
1. Draw a large figure eight starting at A and going around C, crossing at B.

2. Draw a square around F. Draw a square around I. Connect these squares with a straight line.

3. Draw a straight line from E to D, passing through B.

4. Write the figure one between A and H. Write the figure three between F and B. Write the figure two between E and I. Using a straight line, connect one with two, passing through three.

5. Starting at H, use a broken line (- - - - -) and mark the way to D. Continuing with a broken line, mark the way to G from D. From G mark to H. The design should have the shape of a triangle.

6. Write the figure three between G and C. Write the figure four between I and C. Using an oblong circle, enclose these two numbers.

B. Introduction to the Class: On your drawing paper write the letters in the same positions you see them on the board.

Then read the directions given. Draw whatever the directions tell you.

(Note: the vocabulary can be adjusted to meet the needs of the pupils. The vocabulary should be discussed when the papers are checked.)

The child's finished paper should look like this:

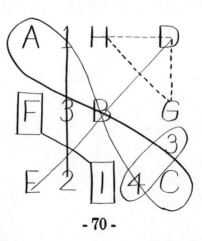

C. Variations: (Grades 4-8)

1. Spatial Image Directions

a. Preparation and Materials: Children will need drawing paper and pencils.

Draw on the board the dots in the positions as shown below. List the directions given.

Example:

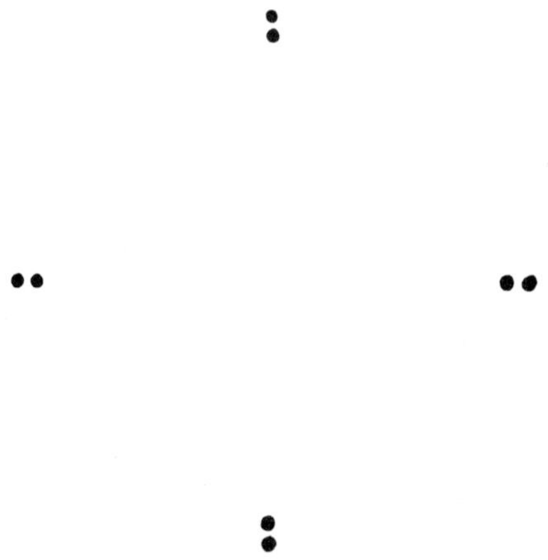

. :

.. ..

. :

Directions:

1. To the best of your ability, make a large circle using the dots to guide your work.

2. Within this large circle, draw a square, making the corners touch the circle at four places.

3. Within the square, draw another circle, making it touch the square at four places.

4. With your pencil, shade the area outside the inner circle, and within the square.

5. Within the last circle, draw any geometric figure you wish, but it must be kept within the area of the circle and touch the circle at three or four places.

b. Introduction to the Class: Draw on your paper the dots as you see them on the board. Then read the directions and draw whatever the directions tell you.

(The child's completed paper should look like this:)

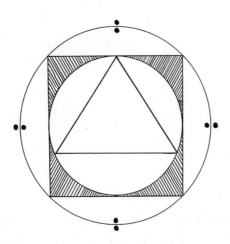

2. Number Game (Grades 4-8)

a. Preparation and Materials: Draw on the board the numbers in the positions shown below. List the directions given.

Children will need drawing paper and pencils.

Example:

$$1 \quad 2 \quad 3$$

$$4 \quad 5 \quad 6$$

$$7 \quad 8 \quad 9$$

Directions:

1. Connect 3, 5, and 7 with a straight line.

2. Connect 7, 8, and 9 with a straight line.

3. Connect 3, 6, and 9 with a straight line.

4. What is the name given the geometric shape made by these straight lines?

5. Draw a circle around each of the following numbers: 1, 2, 4, 5.

6. Connect the circles with a straight line starting at 1, passing through 2, drawing on through 5, connecting 5 with 4, and ending at 1.

7. What is the name of this geometric shape?

8. Which figures would you connect with straight lines to make the largest square possible?

   b. **Introduction to the Class:** Write the numbers on your paper in the positions shown on the board. Then follow the written directions given. Numbers 4, 7, and 8 are questions. Write the answers to these questions in the lower left-hand corner of your paper.

(Child's completed paper should look like this:)

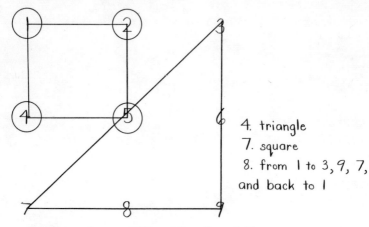

4. triangle
7. square
8. from 1 to 3, 9, 7, and back to 1

3. Drawing a Map (Grades 4-8)

a. Preparation and Materials: Children will need drawing paper, pencils, and crayons.

List on the board the directions given below:

1. On your paper, use the letter N for north, S for south, E for east, and W for west. Place these letters where you would find them on a map.

2. Between west and east, there is a street. Draw two parallel lines, about an inch apart, running from west to east.

3. On the north side of this street, the traffic moves west. Using arrows, show the direction of the traffic on the north side of the street.

4. On the south side of the street, the traffic moves west to east. Using arrows, show the way the traffic moves.

5. There is a city park on the south side of the street. Write **park** in this area.

6. There are five houses on the north side of the street. Use a symbol of your own choosing to represent the houses.

b. Introduction to the Class: Please read the directions on the board, and draw exactly what the directions tell you.

(Child's completed paper should look like this:)

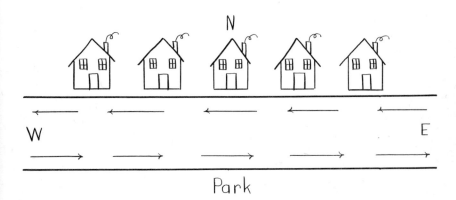

SEATWORK ACTIVITIES
SECTION 4
CREATIVE WRITING

1. SEQUENCE FOR DEVELOPING INDEPENDENT WRITING SKILLS (Grades 1-2)

A. Step 1

1. Preparation and Materials: Children will need drawing paper, pencils, and crayons.

Divide the board into sections. Draw a picture illustrating a prepositional phrase in each section, (a ball **under** a chair, an airplane **over** a house, etc.). In each section, write a question about that picture.

Example:

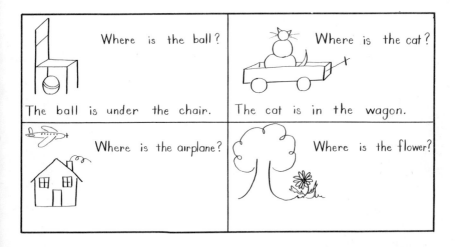

2. Introduction to the Class: I have divided the board into four sections. In each section, is a picture, and a question about that picture.

First fold your paper in half each way so that you will have four sections, just as I have on the board. Then draw the picture and write the question in one section.

Let's look at the first section together. It shows

a chair and a ball. The question asks, "Where is the ball?" How would you answer that question, Jimmy? Can you answer it **in a complete sentence?** (Insist that the answers be given in complete sentences.) Yes, the ball is under the chair. I will write that under the question. (The teacher writes, "The ball is under the chair," as in the above illustration).

You may do the same in each of the other squares. First draw the picture and write the question. Then write the answer to that question in a complete sentence.

Please use your pencil for all the writing, and save your crayons for the pictures.

B. Step 2

After the children have had several experiences with Step 1, draw the same type of pictures on the board, but omit the questions. Ask the children to write one sentence about each picture.

C. Step 3

Ask the children to draw whatever they wish in each square, and to write one sentence about each picture. When the children have mastered this latter skill, they will be ready to begin writing independent stories which are several sentences in length.

2. INDIVIDUAL STORY BOOKS (Grades 1-3)

A. Preparation and Materials: Each child will need writing paper and a pencil. The teacher will need typewriter, stencils, a duplicating machine, and stapler.

B. Introduction to the Class: I know your parents would enjoy reading the nice stories you write in school. So today, after you write your stories, I will type them on a stencil and mimeograph them so that each of you will be able to have a book of stories written by yourself and your classmates to show your parents.

After the pages are mimeographed, I will ask some of you to help me staple the pages together. You can each read your story from your book to the class before you take it home.

3. GROUP STORY BOOKS (Grades 1-3)

A. Preparation and Materials: Each child will need a pencil and writing paper. Perhaps a committee would enjoy making a cover and backing sheet for the book. You will need a paper punch and paper fasteners to use when putting the book together.

B. Introduction to the Class: Today you have asked to write stories about our trip to the post office (or whatever special event has taken place).

When you finish your stories, I will help you fasten them all together to make a book. I will put the book on our reading table. It will be a good record of our trip, and the book will also be fun to read during free time.

C. Variation: You may ask the children to fold drawing paper in half, and paste writing paper in the lower half. They may use the bottom part to write a story, and the top to illustrate the story. These pages may be fastened together to make a book as described above.

Example:

4. LETTER WRITING (Grades 1-8)

During seatwork time, children can write creative thank-you letters, invitations, or letters to convey special information to their parents.

Before the class begins writing, discuss letter form and the general idea the letter should convey. It is also helpful to list special vocabulary, (names, dates, locations, etc.) on the board if the words they will need to use are beyond their present independent spelling ability.

5. BOOK COVERS (Grades 2-8)

A. Preparation and Materials: Children will need drawing paper, crayons, and pencils.

B. Introduction to the Class: Many times we pick up a book to read just because the cover of that book looks interesting. What book do you see in our library that you would like to read because of its interesting cover, John? (After he has selected a book, discuss the interesting features of that cover — the color, design, and action or mood it portrays. If necessary, have the class look at several interesting book covers.)

Today I would like you to make some interesting book covers. Tommy likes stories about jets. Maybe he would like to make a cover for an imaginary book about jets. Mary enjoys dog stories, and perhaps that's what her book cover will be about.

Did you notice that every book cover contained three important parts? First, it told the name of the book. Next, it told the author. You will be the author of your book, so you may put your own name on the cover. Third, it showed an interesting picture about the story.

You may fold your paper in half to make your book cover. Put the fold at the left side, so it will open like a book. Then draw and label your book cover. When you finish, you may pin your covers on the bulletin board to show the class what kind of story you would like to write or read about.

C. Variations: If the paper is folded to size, children would enjoy making covers to protect and beautify their reading books. Or, at a later date, another seatwork period may be used to write a story to staple inside the covers. These books could then be placed on the reading table for free time reading. Or they may be read aloud to the class and then taken home as small gifts to parents.

6. GROUP WRITING (Grades 1-8)

A. Preparation and Materials: Blackboard and chalk. Committee will need drawing paper and writing paper to copy the story.

B. Introduction to the Class: As each situation

is completely different, it would be impracticable to give a standard introduction. First discuss the general topic, and ask what kinds of things children would like to include in their original story or poem.

Then ask, "How shall our story start? What should come next? How shall our story end?" Write the story or poem on the board as children dictate.

Each child may then make a copy of the group-composed story to take home or a committee may copy and illustrate the story. A cumulative book can be made by fastening these pages together as, from time to time, they are composed. The book can then be used for leisure-time reading.

7. CORRELATED ART AND CREATIVE WRITING (Grades 1-8)

Children should be encouraged to write creative stories to be displayed with their art work. For example, at the beginning of the year when the children paint pictures to show something special they did during the summer, they could use seatwork time to write stories about their pictures.

If children paint abstract pictures, they could write about a make-believe fairy land, a make-believe garden, a make-believe space trip, or whatever their particular picture suggests.

If children made clay animals, they might write a story using their animals as central characters. If they made wooden boats or planes, they might write of trips they would like to take in their toys.

These stories could be displayed with the art objects which inspired their creation.

8. COMPLETING SENTENCES (Grades 2-6)

A. Preparation and Materials: Children will need writing paper and pencils.

On the board, list beginnings of several sentences. Put a blank line at the end of each to indicate that it is incomplete.

Example:

1. Are you _____?
2. That little bird _____.
3. Where is _____?
4. One day, I _____.
5. I like to _____.
6. Is that _____?

B. Introduction to the Class: I have written the beginnings of some sentences on the board, but none of the sentences are complete. What do you think you could add to the end of No. 1 to make it a complete sentence, Linda? Do you have a different idea, Phillip? (Let several children orally complete the sentence so the class can see that it can be finished in a variety of ways.)

Now you may take your paper and pencils and complete each sentence in a way you feel to be interesting.

9. ANSWERING QUESTIONS

A. Preparation and Materials: On the board, list a number of questions about a story the class has read, a unit they are studying, a trip they have taken, etc.

Children will need pencil and paper.

B. Introduction to the Class: On the board, you see a number of questions. Read the first question to yourself. Think what the answer should be. Then write your answer **in a complete sentence.** Finish the others in the same way.

SEATWORK ACTIVITIES
SECTION 5
MISCELLANEOUS

1. FINDING WORDS (Grades 2-8)

A. Preparation and Materials: Write a story title (or a long word) on the board. Children will need writing paper and pencils.

B. Introduction to the Class: I have written the word "Rumplestiltskin" on the board. We all enjoyed the story very much, and today we will have some fun with the name of that story.

I would like to see how many words you can make using the letters in the word, "Rumplestiltskin." You can use a letter in each word only as many times as it appears in the word, "Rumplestiltskin," but the letter or letters can be used over again when you make a new word. (For example, one "n" could be used per word, as that letter appears only once in "Rumplestiltskin," but "n" can be used again when needed in a new word). Let's see if we can find a few words together.

After children have suggested several possible words and understand how to proceed, they may take out pencil and paper and begin composing their individual lists.

Example:

up	until	it	lump	kiss
still	rest	tip	net	spit
ski	pen	miss	pet	plum
is	tin	step	met	list
skip	men	lip	sir	spit
skin	in	sip	sum	tilt
stilt	kin	set	ten	pull
pin	sit	less	run	plump

2. CALENDARS (Grades 1-3)

A. Preparation and Materials: Mimeograph calendar sheets such as that given in the example below. Display a large calendar for that month. Children will need pencils and crayons.

Example:

This month is _____

B. Introduction to the Class: Today we are going to make calendars like this one at the front of the room. I have given each of you a mimeographed sheet. At the top is a space for a picture. Below this is a space for you to write the name of this month. (The teacher should then write the name of the month on the board).

We have studied the names of the days of the week and how to spell them. You may write these names, in their proper order, in the spaces at the top of each column. (The teacher should illustrate on the board).

Next you may fill in the numbers for the days of the month just as you see them on our big calendar. When you finish, you may each take your calendar home. You may hang it in your bedroom and cross the days off, or write in special notations just as we do on our big calendar at school.

3. WRITING NUMBERS (Grade 1-2)

A. Preparation and Materials: Children will need drawing paper, pencils, and crayons.

Divide the board in squares. In each square, write a number from one to ten. Write the Arabic numeral.

B. Introduction to the Class: First you will need to fold your drawing paper into thirds each way. Now let's look at the first square on the board. The number "6" is written in it. I would like you to draw six objects in that square. Under your picture, write the word **six,** and then the name of the objects you have drawn. For example, if you drew 6 boats in the first square, you would write **six boats** under your picture. (The teacher illustrates.) Then go on and do the other squares in the same way. Use your crayons for the pictures, but do all the writing with your pencils.

Example:

On Board

6	3	4
9	2	7
1	8	5

Child's Paper

(six boats)	(three apples)	(four trees)
six boats	three apples	four trees
	etc.	

4. MATCHING NUMBERS (Grade 1)

A. Preparation and Materials: Children will need writing paper and pencils. Divide the board into two columns. In each column, list six Arabic numerals, and across from them, list the written words for these numbers.

B. Introduction to the Class: Today I would like to see how well you can match these numbers to the words which say the same numbers. First fold your paper in half to make two columns. Then write the six numbers along the left side of your paper just as I have done on the board. Next write the column of number-words as you see them on the board in the second column. Then draw a line to match each number to its proper number-word, like this. (The teacher illustrates by matching one pair on the board).

When you finish one column, go right ahead and do the second column in the same way.

Example:

1	three	7	eleven
2	six	8	nine
3	two	9	seven
4	five	10	twelve
5	one	11	ten
6	four	12	eight

5. MATCHING DAYS OF THE WEEK WITH THEIR ABBREVIATED FORM (Grade 2)

A. Preparation and Materials: Children will need writing paper and pencils. Along the left side of the board, list the names of the days of the week, in their proper order, one below another. Beside this, list the abbreviations in mixed-up order.

B. Introduction to the Class: Today I would like to see how well you can match the names of the days of the week with their abbreviated forms. First list the names of the days of the week along the left side of your paper. Next write the column of abbreviations, just as you see them on the board.

Then draw a line to match each weekday name to its abbreviated form like this. (The teacher illustrates by matching one pair of words on the board).

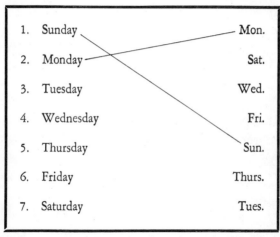

C. Variation: Ask children to match names of the months of the year with abbreviated forms of these words.

6. CROSSWORD PUZZLES (Grades 2-8)

A. Preparation and Materials: Duplicate a crossword puzzle sheet for each member of the class. Vary the complexity of the puzzle to fit the level of your group. Lower grades would find a puzzle with answers written across only (such as shown below), of sufficient challenge. Higher grades could work a traditional crossword puzzle with answers written both across and down.

Example:

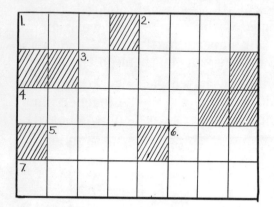

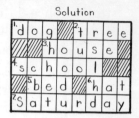

Solution

1. It says "bow-wow."
2. Apples grow on this.
3. You live in this.
4. You learn to read and write here.
5. You sleep in this.
6. You wear this on your head.
7. This is the day of the week after Friday.

B. Introduction to the Class: I have given each of you a crossword-puzzle sheet. At the top of the page are many squares. At the bottom of the page are several sentences.

Let's look at the first sentence together. What does it say, Bob? Yes, "It says 'bow-wow'." What do you think that sentence describes, Sue? Of course, a dog.

What is the number of the sentence? Yes, number one. Now find the number one in the puzzle squares. Put the first letter of **dog** in that square. Finish the word by putting one letter in each of the following squares.

Now look at the second sentence. Where would you write what this sentence describes, Sally? Yes, you will put the first letter in the square with the "2" in it, and one letter in each of the following squares.

(Continue in this fashion until you are sure the children understand how to work the puzzle. If necessary, draw a large puzzle on the board and work the entire puzzle with the class. Then erase the board before the children begin their individual puzzles.)

7. ALPHABETIZING (Grades 1-2)

A. Preparation and Materials: List on the board, one word beginning with each letter of the alphabet. Put these words in three columns, and list them in no particular order. Children will need pencils and writing paper.

Example:

good	hello	elephant
baby	jump	ice
look	dog	kite
Mother	take	new
apple	very	over
zoo	x-ray	play
you	under	we
ride	for	queen
Sally	come	

B. Introduction to the Class: First I would like you to fold your writing paper into thirds to make three columns.

I would like you to arrange the words you see on the board in alphabetical order. That means that the word beginning with "a" will come first, next will come the word beginning with "b," then the word beginning with "c," and so on.

To do this work, you will first have to think what letter comes first in the alphabet. What letter is that, Mildred? Yes, "a." Now can you find a word on the board which begins with "a," Mike? Yes, **apple.** So the first word you will write on your paper will be **apple.**

What is the next letter of the alphabet, Greg? Yes, "b." Can you find a word on the board that begins with "b," Carol? Yes, **baby,** so the next word you will write will be **baby.**

What is the very last word you will write, Barbara? Yes, **zoo,** because **zoo** starts with "z," and "z" is the last letter of the alphabet.

Are there any questions? Then you may begin.

8. PLAYING IN THE RAIN (Grade 1)

A. Preparation and Materials: Mimeograph sheets showing an umbrella and raindrops as illustrated on the following page. Write a letter in each section of the umbrella, and a matching letter in each of the raindrops.

Give each child one of these mimeographed sheets. Each child will also need a pencil.

Example:

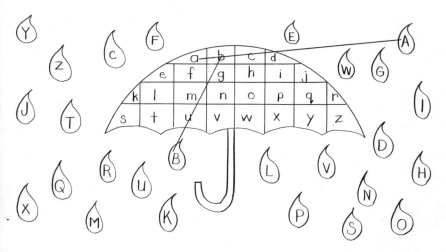

B. Introduction to the Class: Since today is such a rainy day, I thought you might enjoy playing in the rain. There is a letter written on each raindrop, and one written in each section of the umbrella.

I would like you to find a letter in a raindrop, and the same letter on the umbrella. Then match the letters which are the same by drawing a line between them. The line will show you where that raindrop will hit the umbrella!

Can you find where each raindrop will land?

GAMES
SECTION 1
PHONETIC ANALYSIS

1. MEMORY (Grades 2-4)

A. Preparation and Materials: Each child should have writing paper and a pencil. The teacher will need a tray and toys or small items to place on it. By careful selection of the items on the tray, the teacher can provide drill in writing almost any phonetic sounds.

For example, if the "ack-ick-ock" sounds were being studied, the tray might contain such material as:

sock	tack	sack	lock
stick	clock	block	jacks

Or for stress on the three-letter words the tray might contain:

fan	hat	cup	car	pan	nut
pin	gum	box	pen	top	map

B. Introduction to the Class: Today we're going to play a game to find out how well you can remember what you see. The game will also show me how well you can spell.

I have a tray with several things on it. I'm going to show each of you this tray for just a short time (about 10 seconds). After each of you has seen the tray, I will tell you to take your pencil and write down the names of as many things as you remember seeing on the tray.

Your answers must be spelled correctly to be counted right. But that shouldn't be too hard for you because all the names of the things on this tray contain a sound we have been studying this week. (Teacher then writes the letters for the sounds on the board, "ack-ick-ock," for example, and children review these sounds.)

You may take out your pencils and papers now, but you won't begin writing until everyone has seen the tray. I'll tell you when to begin. The person with the most answers correctly spelled will be the winner. (Teacher then passes the tray, allowing each child to see it for about 10 seconds. When all have finished looking, she should say, "You may begin writing now.")

2. GUESS WHAT (Grades 2-4)

A. Preparation and Materials: Children will need writing paper and pencils. This game is on much the same order as "Memory" (see GAMES, Section 1, Number 1), but rather than placing the items on a tray, each one is put into a separate candy sack. The sack should then be stapled shut and numbered.

For the "ar-or" unit, each sack might contain one of the following:

cork	toy car	jar	scarf	fork
corn	playing card	horn	marble	yarn

For study in the long vowels, each sack must contain one of these:

rope	candy cane	toy plane	pipe
dime	toy rake	roll of tape	bone

B. Introduction to the Class: Boys and girls, you have become so good at remembering what you see in the "Memory" game (see GAMES, Section 1, Number 1) that I've had to find a new way to try and fool you. I have put one item into each of these sacks (teacher holds up one of the sacks), and I have stapled each of the sacks shut so that you can't see inside.

I am going to pass these sacks around the room, and you can feel, pinch, shake, or smell each sack;

and write down what you think is inside. First number your paper from 1 to 10 (or whatever number of sacks there are). Look at the number on the sack. Write your answer by the same number on your paper as you see on the sack. After you have written, you may pass the sack to your neighbor. Remember, your answers must be spelled correctly to be counted right. The person with the most correct answers will be our winner.

The names of the items in these sacks all contain one of the sounds we have been studying this week. (Teacher then writes the letters for the sounds on the board, "ar-or," for example, and children review the sounds.)

You may take out your pencils now. Are you ready? (Teacher then begins passing the sacks.)

3. I SPY (Grades 1-2)

A. Preparation and Materials: None.

B. Introduction to the Class. We have been studying beginning consonants and the sounds they make. Today we are going to play a game that will show me how well you remember these sounds. The game is called "I Spy."

One of you will be "it." You will come to the front of the room and tell us the beginning sound of something you spy in the room. For example, you might say, "I spy something that starts with "w." Then we might guess the windows, the woodwork, the walls, etc. The person who guesses correctly may be the next "it."

Are there any questions? Then let's begin.

4. SHOW ME (Grades 1-2)

A. Preparation and Materials: Each child will

need 26 cards, each one showing a different letter of the alphabet. To make these cards, rule tagboard into 3" squares. Appoint a committee to cut the squares and to write the letters to make a set of alphabet cards for each child in the class. Ask them to put a rubber band around each complete set.

The following list contains words beginning with each letter of the alphabet, which the teacher might pronounce during the game:

good	even	face	kite
jump	look	ice	news
over	Mother	picture	top
queen	summer	radio	under
wagon	xylophone	very	after
zoo	your	corn	baby
	dog	hat	

B. Introduction to the Class: I have given each of you a set of 26 cards. One letter of the alphabet is on each card. Would you put your cards, face up and in alphabetical order, on your desk, please? You will need to make several rows, so put "A" in the upper left-hand corner of your desk to begin.

Now I will pronounce a word. (See list above.) Listen to the beginning sound of that word. Look on your desk and find the letter which says that beginning sound. Pick it up and hold it against your chest so that no one can see the letter. When I say "Show me," hold your card up so that I can see it.

I will go very slowly at first, but later I will begin to go faster, so you will need to listen carefully and do your very best thinking.

C. Variations: This game was designed as a quick test to discover those who need further drill in the consonant sounds. However, its variations are limitless. The children may have a set of cards showing just the vowels. The teacher could then pronounce three-letter words, and the children could show what vowel sound they heard in that word. Or, they might have a set of consonant blends, endings, or parts of words, and show what sound the pronounced word contained.

5. HOPSCOTCH (Grades 2-3)

A. Preparation and Materials: Write at the top of the board the letters for the sounds to be stressed. Below this, divide the board into squares and draw in each square a picture of an object, the name of which contains one of these sounds. (See figure 1.)

Example:

an - ap - at

Consonant Blends

| Figure 1 | Figure 2 |

You may prefer to make hopscotch squares on large sheets of tagboard which can be stored for re-use.

Figure 2 shows hopscotch squares in which children need tell the stressed sound rather than spell the complete word. This is often necessary when words containing the stressed sounds are beyond the children's present independent spelling ability. They will still receive ear training in the stressed sounds.

B. Introduction to the Class: I have drawn several pictures on the board. Each picture is in a square. We are going to play hopscotch in these squares.

Before we begin, let's look at the letters for the sounds written at the top of the board. Say the sounds for the letters that you see, Sally. That's right, "an, ap, and at." Now let's look at the first picture. It is a hat. Which of those three sounds do you hear in the word **hat,** Mildred? That's right, "at."

What letter would we need to put in front of "at" to spell the complete word, **hat,** David? That's right, "h."

Now can you spell the whole word, **hat,** Billy? Good! Do you think you can hop the rest of the squares in the same way? First tell me which sound you hear, and then spell the complete word. When you have finished, you may choose the next person to play hopscotch.

6. HUMAN SPELLING (Grades 2-6)

A. Preparation and Materials: Break apart two sets of alphabet cards used in "Show Me," (GAMES, Section 1, Number 4). First distribute one complete alphabet set, giving each child one card. If there are more than 26 children in your class, give the remaining children cards from the second set, distributing first the vowel cards; then "t," "r," "b," and the other most frequently used consonants. The children holding cards from the second alphabet set should be instructed to come up only if their letter is used **twice** in the word being spelled.

B. Introduction to the Class: I have given each of you a card. One letter of the alphabet is on that card. I am going to pronounce a word. If the letter you hold is in that word, you may come to the front of the room. The other children having a letter in that word will come up, too. Each of you will hold your card in front of you so the class may see it. You will arrange yourselves in the proper order to spell the word correctly.

For example, if I said **run,** (teacher writes **run** on the board), the children holding "r," "u," and "n" would come to the front of the room. Who would stand first? Yes, "r." Who would stand in the middle? "U," that's right. Who would stand at the end? Yes, "n" would be last. Let's try doing that. (Children practice spelling **run**).

Are there any questions? Then are we ready to try spelling some different words? (The teacher then begins pronouncing words within the children's present independent spelling ability.)

7. TEAM SPELLING (Grades 2-8)

A. Preparation and Materials: Divide the board into four sections. Number the sections from one to four. Have chalk and an eraser available in each section. Have a list of spelling words to pronounce for the teams.

B. Introduction to the Class: Today we are going to play a spelling game. We shall need four teams for this game, so let's count off by 4's. Will the 1's please sit in the front row (or go to whatever spot you designate), the 2's sit in the second row, etc.?

I have divided the blackboard into four sections, one section for each team. The number in each section tells which team will use that space.

Will the first person from each team please go to the board? Now I will pronounce one of our spelling words. Each of you will write that word on the board. The first person to finish the word correctly wins a point for his team. At the end of the playing time, the team with the most points will be the winner, and may be excused first for recess (or be given some other special privilege).

8. COUNT TO TEN (Grades 2-6)

A. Preparation and Materials: Display a chart of all the sounds studied thus far in the phonics class.

B. Introduction to the Class: We shall need to form a circle for our game today; then we shall sit on the floor.

A list of the letters for all the sounds we have studied so far this year is on our chart rack. One person will be "it." He will choose a pair of these letters, **ack-ick,** for example; then he will walk around the inside of the circle and tap each of us on the head. He will say one of these sounds as he taps each child.

Suddenly he will stop by one of us, name one of the two sounds and begin to count to 10. The other child must name a word containing that sound before "it" can count to 10.

If he can do this, he may be the new "it" and choose a new pair of sounds and start again.

It will be easier for you if you think of two words as soon as "it" chooses his sounds; then you will be ready if "it" stops by **you!**

9. SIGNAL THE SOUND (Grades 2-6)

A. Preparation and Materials: Prepare a list of

words containing the three sounds you wish to stress. Write these three sounds on the blackboard (**ing, ight, old,** for example).

B. Introduction to the Class: I have written on the board the letters for the three sounds we are studying now, **ing, ight,** and **old.** Now we shall need to think of a signal to use each time we hear one of these sounds. For **ing,** let's wave our hands high in the air. Would you try that, please?

For **ight,** let's fold our hands in our laps. May I see you do that? For **old,** we could put our hands on our shoulders. Would you try that, please? (The second time children play this game, they will be able to choose their own signals.)

Now I will pronounce a word. I want you to give the signal for the sound you hear in that word. If I said **ring,** what signal would you use, Mary? That's right, you would wave your hands in the air. You can hear **ing** in **ring,** and waving our hands is the signal for **ing.** (Review the other two sounds and signals in the same manner.)

Now we are ready to begin. I will go very slowly at first, but later I will say the words more quickly, so you will need to listen and think carefully.

C. Variations: As the class becomes more advanced, you may ask them to signal homophones ("ay-ai," "oy-oi") to distinguish which would be used in the particular word you pronounce.

10. BALL TOSS (Grades 2-4)

A. Preparation and Materials: Display a list of the letters for all the sounds studied thus far in the phonics class. Supply a large rubber ball.

B. Introduction to the Class: For the game of

"Ball Toss," we shall need to form a circle. One child will be "it," and he will have this rubber ball. He will name a sound we have studied, and then toss the ball to someone in the circle. The child must name a word containing that sound as he catches the ball.

For example, if I said "oy" and tossed the ball to you, what might you say as you caught the ball, Tommy? That's right, **toy.**

If you catch the ball **and** say a correct word, you will be the next "it"; but if you miss either the ball or the word, you must sit in the center. You can go back to the circle as soon as someone else misses and comes to take your place in the center.

11. WHAT AM I? (Grades 2-3)

A. Preparation and Materials: Rule tagboard into 2″ x 4″ cards. Make a list of three-letter words (nouns). Appoint a committee to cut the cards and to write one of the words on each card. Make one card for each child in the class.

B. Introduction to the Class: Each of you has a card on which is written the name of an animal or toy. You will want to put your card face down on your desk so that no one can see it.

One child will bring his card up to the front of the class. He will not let us see the word, but he will give us some clues about it. Maybe his card says, "pig." Then he might say, "I am fat. I say, 'Oink.' I have a curly tail. What am I?" Then he may call on someone to **spell** the answer to his riddle, "P - I - G."

The child who can correctly spell the word may be the next "it."

12. RIDDLES (Grades 2-3)

A. Preparation and Materials: Prepare a list of words which contain the sounds you wish to stress. You can easily make up the riddles as you go along. As children guess each riddle, write the answer on the board and underline the stressed part.

This game is designed for ear training, and can be adapted to almost any sounds.

B. Introduction to the Class: This week we have been studying the sounds "ai" and "ay" (or whatever sounds are currently being studied). I have some riddles to ask you. The answers to my riddles have either the "ai" or "ay" sounds in them. Can you guess my riddles?

Sample Riddles:

1. It falls from a cloud. (rain)

2. You can carry water in this. (pail)

3. You do this in church. (pray)

4. You put prisoners in this. (jail)

5. It means you are happy. (gay)

6. Boats do this. (sail)

7. A dog wags this when he is happy. (tail)

8. Cows eat this. (hay)

13. DAILY NEWS (Grades 1-3)

A. Preparation and Materials: None. This activity may be used with any material you may wish to put on the board.

B. Introduction to the Class: Today, as you tell

me your news and I write it on the board, we will play a game. Now and then I will stop writing, and call on someone to spell the next word for me.

14. WORD-O (Grades 2-4)

A. Preparation and Materials: Fold 9″ x 12″ manila drawing paper into 12 squares, and distribute one sheet to each member of the class. Cut colored paper into 1″ squares to be used as markers. Give a committee one envelope for each member of the class, and ask that they put 12 markers in each envelope. They may then distribute the envelopes to the class.

Prepare a list of about 20 words containing the sounds you wish to stress. Only one word should be listed for each stressed sound.

A sample list of consonant blend words is:

shoe	sled	block	broom
train	plane	drum	present
grapes	store	clock	wheel
flag	chicken	spoon	frog
crib	swing	skates	glass

Write these words on the board, and keep a copy to guide you in writing the sounds once the game begins.

The illustrated sheets and envelopes containing the markers may be collected and saved for re-use at the end of the playing time.

Once children have become very familiar with these sounds, they may wish to make cards illustrating new sounds. The list of words could be placed on the board, and children could illustrate their new sheets during seatwork time. The same envelopes and markers can, of course, be used throughout the year.

This game is especially good for cumulative review.

B. Introduction to the Class: Each of you has a sheet of drawing paper which is folded into 12 squares. You also have an envelope which contains 12 colored markers. Will you please put the envelope at the top of your desk for now?

We have been studying the sounds of double consonants, and I have written some words containing these sounds on the board. Let's read the list together. (Children read the list aloud.)

Now you may take out your crayons. You may choose any 12 of these words, and illustrate one in each square of your paper. Try to mix up your pictures so they are not in the same order as the words on the board.

Have you finished your pictures? If you have finished, I will erase the board.

Now you may take the colored markers from the envelope and lay them beside your picture sheet. I am going to write a double consonant on the board. If you have a picture on your card which begins with that sound, you may put a marker on it.

If I wrote "fl" on the board, which picture would you mark, Susan? That's right, the flag. But if you do not have the flag pictured, you cannot put on any marker.

As soon as you have put markers on a complete row of pictures, either across or down, you say "Word-o." I will help you check your card to make sure you have marked it correctly. If your card is marked correctly, you have won. Then we begin a new game.

15. ACTING OUT "MAGICAL e" (Grades 2-3)

A. Preparation and Materials: Use the same cards as in "Human Spelling" (see GAMES, Section 1, No. 6, page 106), but take out the regular vowel cards. In their place, put two cards for each vowel, one marked long, and one marked short. Also add one card which has a red "e" written on it. This will be the "Magical e" card. Distribute one of these cards to each member of the class.

B. Introduction to the Class: The game we are going to play now is something like the "Human Spelling" game, but the cards are a little different. We have **two** cards for each vowel, one marked short, and the other marked long. Let's review the meaning of the long and short vowel marks, and the sounds of the long and short vowels before we begin our game. (Here insert a short review lesson.)

Now I am going to pronounce a word, just as I did in our other spelling game. But this time we will need to be very careful with the vowels. We will have to be sure the children holding the long-vowel cards come up only when they hear their long-vowel sound in the word I pronounce, and the children holding the short-vowel cards come up only when they hear their short-vowel sound.

For example, if I said **not,** which letters would come to the front of the room? Yes, the "n," "o," and "t." But **which** "o"? That's right, the **short** "o," because "o" has a short sound in the word **not.** Will those letters come up here, please?

Who is holding the red "e"? That is our "Magical e." Will you come up and stand at the end of our word? What is the word they spell now, class? That's right, **note.** But what is wrong with the way they have it spelled? Yes, the "o" must be a **long** "o" now. Will the person holding the long "o" card please come up and take the place of the short "o"?

Proceed in this fashion, acting out the change in the preceding vowel when "Magical e" is added to the end of the word. Children might act out such changes as:

pin to pine	hat to hate
fin to fine	cut to cute
us to use	Tim to time
hop to hope	tap to tape
cap to cape	can to cane
Sam to same	rip to ripe

C. Variation: (Grades 4-8) Use the same cards described above, but play the "Human Spelling" described in GAMES, Section 1, Number 6, p. 106. Children will need to be careful **which** vowels come to the front of the room to spell the pronounced word. Also, the child holding the "Magical e" card should come up only when the word ends with a silent "e" **and** the preceding vowel is long. For example, in the words **there** and **where** the final "e" is **not** magical.

This variation, of course, requires added skill. It requires greater discrimination of sounds than does "Human Spelling," and the children will not have the teacher's help in verbalizing each thought process as in "Acting out 'Magical e'."

16. ALPHABET (Grades 2-6)

A. Preparation and Materials: Rule tagboard into 2" x 4" cards. Appoint a committee to cut the squares and to write upon each card a sound that has been studied by the class. There should be one less card than there are members of the class.

B. Introduction to the Class: Each of you has a card showing a letter for a sound we have studied this year. But if you'll notice, Steve has no card. And I am going to move his chair away so that he has no place to sit.

Steve is "it," and he will say "Cards up." Then each of you will hold your card so that he can read it. He will call out two sounds, **saying** the sounds rather than naming the letters in them. The children holding the letter cards for the sounds he names must quickly change seats. Steve will try to get one of the empty chairs first. Whoever is left without a chair will be the next "it."

If he calls "Alphabet," everyone must change places.

17. WHO SAID THAT? (Grades 2-6)

A. Preparation and Materials: Use the same letter cards as in the "Alphabet" game (see GAMES, Section 1, Number 16, p. 106).

B. Introduction to the Class: I have the same letter cards that we used in our "Alphabet" game, but today we are going to play a new game with them. One child will be "it." He will put his head down on his desk.

Next I will hold up a card and point to a child in the room. That child will **say** (not spell) the sound of the letter written on the card. He may use his own voice or a funny voice, but we must be able to understand the sound he says.

Then "it" will put up his head and try to guess who said the sound. He may have three guesses.

If he can guess, the child who said the sound will be the next "it." If he cannot guess, he himself must be "it" again.

18. SOUND TEAMS (Grades 2-6)

A. Preparation and Materials: Divide the blackboard into four sections. Number the sections from 1 to 4. In each section, write the sounds being currently studied, **ing, ight, old,** and **y,** for example. The same sounds should be written in each section. Provide chalk and an eraser in each section.

Prepare a list of words containing these sounds. For the sounds given above, the list might contain such words as:

funny	bring	told	light	happy
bright	sing	finger	sold	sleepy
cold	hold	ring	baby	night

B. Introduction to the Class: For our game, today, we will need four teams. Will you please count off by 4's? Will the 1's please sit in the front row, the 2's in the second row, etc.? (Or go to whatever spot you designate).

The blackboard is divided into four sections. The number in each section tells which team will use that space. The sounds we have been studying this week, **ing, ight, old,** and **y,** are written in each section.

One member from each team will go to the

board. I will pronounce a word which contains one of these sounds. The first child to point to the letter for the sound he hears will win a point for his team. He may draw a mark on the board to show that his team has won a point.

Then a new member from each team will go to the board, and we begin again. At the end of the playing time, the team with the most points wins. The children on that team may be my helpers when we get ready for our art lesson this afternoon. (Or be first to line up for recess, etc.).

19. SOUND ALIKE (Grades 3-6)

A. Preparation and Materials: Rule tagboard into 3" x 6" cards. Appoint a committee to cut the cards. Letter the cards in homophonic pairs. (The letters for one sound only are written on each card.) Two or more cards may show the letters for the same sound but the sound will be spelled differently on each card.

Some of the groups of letters which might be used are:

ow — ou	y — e	er — ir — ur
oy — oi	ow — oa	ai — ay — a
ew — oo	j — g	ea — ee — e
c — s	y — i	

Ask the committee to punch holes in the upper corners of each card, and to tie string through the holes to make a loop. Hang one of these cards around the neck of each child.

Keep a list of sounds used, to call during the game.

Provide a ten-pin.

B. Introduction to the Class: For our "Sound Alike" game we will need to form a circle. In the center of the circle is a ten-pin. Each of you has a card with the letter or letters for the sound written on it. Someone else in the circle has a card with different letters which sound just like yours. Sometimes **three** people have different letters for the same sound!

I will call a sound. If your letter or letters can make that sound, you will run to the center, take the pin, and try to get it "home" to your place in the circle before any of the others with the letters for the same sound can get it. Then you will win a point.

If someone else takes the pin before you, and you can tap him before he gets into his place, he will not receive a point.

You will each keep track of your own points. The person with the most points at the end of the playing time wins.

20. PHONETIC RELAY (Grades 2-6)

A. Preparation and Materials: Divide the blackboard into 4 sections. Number the sections from 1 to 4. List the letters for eight phonetic sounds (or enough to make one sound for each team member) in each section, one letter combination below another. For example, the teacher might list **oy, ick, ell, ight, is, er, ow,** and **ea** in each section.

Draw a chalk line on the floor ten feet away from each section. Provide chalk and an eraser at each section of the board.

Example:

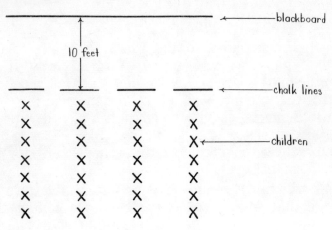

B. Introduction to the Class: We will need four teams for our "Phonetic Relay." Will you count off by 4's, please? I have marked four chalk lines on the floor, ten feet from the blackboard. Will each team stand in a row behind one of those lines, please?

The board is divided into 4 sections, one section for each team. The number in each section tells which team will use that space. On each section, I have listed the letters for 8 sounds which we have been studying.

The first person on each team has a piece of chalk. He will walk up to the board, and beside the letter for the first sound he will write any word he can think of which contains that sound. Then he will walk back and give the chalk to the next person on his team. That person will walk up and write a word by the second letter, and so on, until your team has completed a word by each letter. When you have finished, every person on your team should raise his hand. Then I will know you are done.

The words must be spelled correctly to be counted right. The first team to complete their words correctly will be the winner.

21. THUMBS UP (Grades 3-6)

A. Prepare a list of the letters for sounds which the class has studied thus far in their phonics class.

B. Introduction to the Class: I have a list of the sounds we have studied this year. I am going to write the letters for one of these sounds on the board, and then I will pronounce a word. If the word I say contains the sound of the letters I wrote on the board, put your thumbs up. If it does not contain the letters for that sound, put your thumbs down.

Julia, if I wrote "le" on the board (teacher writes) and then said **candle,** how would you put your thumbs? That's right, you'd put them up. You can hear the "le" sound in can**dle.**"

How would you put your thumbs if I wrote "ay" (teacher writes) and said **jumping,** Jerry? That's right, you'd put them down, because there is no "ay" sound in **jumping.**

We will all stand, and we will all put our thumbs up or down together. If I see someone who missed, that person must sit down. We shall see who can remain standing the longest.

I shall go very slowly at first. But later I shall go faster, so you must listen and think carefully.

22. POEMS, CHORAL READINGS, AND FINGERPLAYS

Children enjoy stories, poems, choral readings, and finger plays which "personalize" phonetic sounds. Books designed for use in speech correction work are a very fine source for such activities.

These same activities fit perfectly into the phonics program in the normal classroom. Some specific books which contain these materials are:

1. Keppie, Elizabeth E. "Speech Improvement Through Choral Speaking." Expression, Boston, 1942.

2. Scott, Louise Binder, and J. J. Thompson. "Talking Time." Webster Publishing Co., St. Louis, 1951. Contains stories, poems, finger plays, and choral readings, stressing most consonant sounds. Also gives directions for making visual aids to accompany some of these activities.

3. Wood, Alice L. "The Jingle Book." Dutton, New York. Contains interesting poems and "nonsense" rhymes, stressing most of the basic sounds.

4. Wood, Alice L. "Sound Games." Dutton, New York, 1948. Games for the very young.

23. GOING ON A TRIP (Grades 1-3)

A. Preparation and Materials: None.

B. Introduction to the Class: Today we are going on an imaginary trip. But before we can go, we must pack our imaginary suitcases! We will pack just certain things.

I shall write the letter "A" on the board. Then the first child might say, "I'm going on a trip, and I'm going to take an apple." **He** can name anything that starts with the letter "A." The next child will try to think of another "A" word to take on his trip. He might say, "I'm going on a trip, and I'm going to take an alligator." Each of you will try to think of a new thing to pack, but the word must start with the letter "A."

As soon as a child misses by not being able to

think of another thing that starts with "A," you will begin to pack "B" things in your suitcases. Are you ready to begin?

C. **Variation:** The first child could name an "A" word, the second child a "B" word, the third child a "C" word, and so on. All children could stand, and when a child missed by not being able to name an item starting with the next letter, he would sit. The last person to remain standing would be the winner.

24. ALPHABET RHYTHM (Grades 3-6)

A. **Preparation and Materials:** None.

B. **Introduction to the Class:** To play "Alphabet Rhythm," we shall need to form a circle and all sit on the floor.

Next we shall practice the rhythm for our game. (Teacher then demonstrates by first lightly hitting her knees with both hands twice, then clapping her hands together twice, then snapping the fingers of first the right hand and then the left hand, in a definite 1-2-3-4-5-6 rhythm. This rhythm pattern is repeated over and over again throughout the game.)

You may watch me, and join in the rhythm when you feel you are able. (As soon as children are able to follow the rhythm pattern, continue the directions for the game.)

Now I think we are ready to begin the game. The first child in the circle will first start our rhythm pattern, and the rest of us will follow him. As he snaps the fingers of his right hand, he will name the first letter of the alphabet, "A," and as he snaps the fingers of his left hand, he will name the sound that letter makes.

Then we will all continue the rhythm pattern together until we come to the next place where we snap our fingers. Then the second child must name the next letter of the alphabet, "B," as he snaps the fingers of his right hand, and the sound that letter makes as he snaps the fingers of his left hand. It will sound like this: (Teacher then demonstrates.)

When a child misses by not being able to name the next letter or sound, he must sit in the center of the circle. The next child then begins with the same letter the previous child missed. As soon as another child misses, the child in the center may return to his place in the circle.

C. Variations: On the first snap of the fingers, a child may name a letter of the alphabet, and as he snaps the second time, he may name a word that begins with that sound.

Or, the teacher may hold flash cards, and on the first snap a child may tell the beginning sound of that word, and on the second snap must name the word itself.

25. STORY PUZZLES (Grades 2-8)

Have the class work together to write a short creative story. Write the story on the blackboard as children dictate, and when it is finished ask several children to read the story aloud to the class.

Then go through the story and erase parts of words — blends, digraphs, initial consonants, endings, etc. Put a line to show where parts have been deleted.

Then ask several children to read the story and "think out loud" the missing letters as they go.

Rather than writing a story especially for this activity, you can use any story or sentences already on the board.

For stress in one particular phonetic sound, erase the letters for just one kind of sound throughout the story, just initial consonants, endings, etc. For a cumulative review, erase a variety of parts.

26. CLIMB THE LADDER (Grades 1-3)

A. Preparation and Materials: Draw a ladder on the board. On each rung, write the letters for a blend sound, or any other letter combination in which children need drill.

Example:

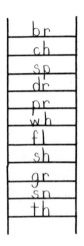

B. Introduction to the Class: Let's go ladder climbing today. To climb this ladder, you must name the sound on each rung as you climb. If you can climb to the top of the ladder, you may be the teacher and point to the rungs as the next child climbs.

27. I HAVE A SECRET (Grades 2-3)

A. Preparation and Materials: Prepare a list of words, one beginning with each letter of the alphabet.

B. Introduction to the Class: I have a secret! I shall pronounce a word, and then call on one of you. You can guess my secret if you can tell the first letter of the word I pronounce.

C. Variations: The teacher could show pictures rather than pronounce words. Or, the list could contain words beginning with letters for blend sounds, and the children would tell what letters make each blend sound. Or, the list could contain words having endings such as **ing, er, est, ed,** etc., and the children could spell the ending of the word the teacher pronounces.

28. LUCKY GAME (Grades 2-8)

A. Preparation and Materials: Fold 9" x 12" manila drawing paper into 16 squares. Cut colored paper into 1" squares for markers. Appoint a committee to count the markers, putting 16 markers into an envelope for each member of the class. Give each child a folded sheet of drawing paper and an envelope of markers. Children will need pencils.

On the board, list foundation-letter combinations, such as the ones given below.

ab	ac	ot	id
ib	eg	ud	om
ob	el	ak	et
ub	an	ed	as
eb	ut	im	ul

B. Introduction to the Class: First let's read together the sounds for the letters written on the board. (Children read sounds together.)

Now I would like you to take your pencils and write the letters for one of these sounds in each square of your paper. Try to mix up the letters, so they are not in the same order on your paper as they are on the board. (When children have completed writing, the teacher should erase the board.)

You may take the colored markers out of your envelopes and lay them beside your cards. I am going to name a sound. When you find the letters for that sound on your card, put a marker on it. When you have marked a complete row of letters, either across or down, call out "Lucky"! We will check your card together. If you have marked your squares correctly, you will be the winner, and we will begin a new game.

(Teacher should write down the letters for each sound as she pronounces it to the class. She can then check the winner's card against this list to make sure the child has marked his card correctly.)

29. PICKING APPLES (Grades 1-3)

A. Preparation and Materials: Draw a large tree, or several trees, on the board. Draw several apples on each tree. On each apple, write vowels, blends, or consonants.

Example:

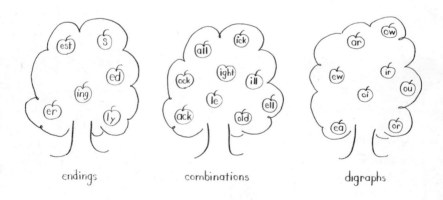

endings   combinations   digraphs

B. Introduction to the Class: We are going to pick apples today. To pick these apples, you must name the sound of the letters written on each one. If you can pick all the apples on this tree, you may be the teacher and point to the apples as the next child "picks."

C. Variations: 1. Children may pick the petals from a daisy:

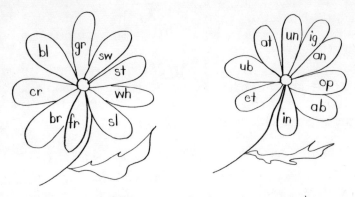

consonant blends   foundation letter combinations

2. Children may see how many carrots the little rabbit can eat:

3. Children may call out what is written on the paper dropped from the airplane:

4. Children may name the rabbits in the magician's hat:

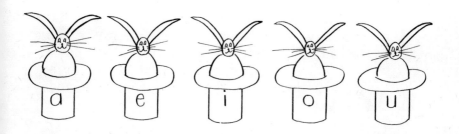

30. SLIDING DOWN THE SOUND SLIDE
(Grades 1-3)

A. Preparation and Materials: Draw a slide on the blackboard. At the top of the slide draw a child and call him "A," or whatever other vowel you wish to stress.

Along the slide write vowel combinations.

Example:

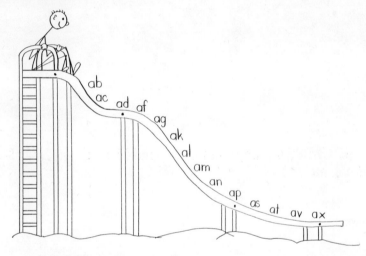

B. Introduction to the Class: Can you make "A" slide all the way down the slide? You can if you can name all the sounds he passes as he slides down. If you can slide "A" all the way down, you may be the teacher and point to the letters for the sounds as the next child slides.

C. Variations: Draw a flight of stairs, and on each step write one of the sounds in which children need drill. Ask the child to run up or down the stairs by naming the sound for the letter on each step.

Example:

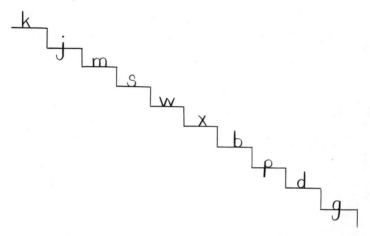

Draw a mountain on the board. Along the mountain, print the letters for the consonants. Put the most difficult ones near the top. At the mountain peak, put a golden egg. An eagle laid the egg at the peak. The pupils may try to climb the mountain to get the golden egg.

Example:

31. PARADE OF THE VOWELS (Grades 2-4)

A. Preparation and Materials: Draw a parade of long vowels on the blackboard. Give each vowel stick legs.

Example:

B. Introduction to the Class: Can you name the vowels in this parade? First tell me the vowel's name, and then tell me the sound that vowel makes when it is long, or give a word containing that long vowel sound, etc.

C. Variation: Using the same idea, have a parade of short vowels.

32. RAILROAD CONDUCTOR GAME (Grades 1-3)

A. Preparation and Materials: Draw a train on the blackboard. Write consonant blends above the smokestack instead of smoke.

Example:

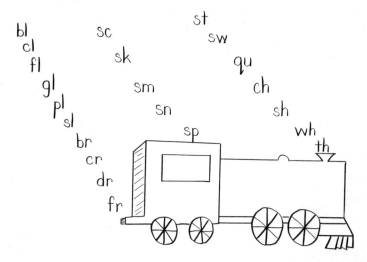

B. Introduction to the Class: Have you ever seen a talking train? Here is one that can talk. It is telling us the names of the stations where it will stop. You may be the conductor on this train and call out the stations where it will stop. (One child at a time can call the names, or the class can call them together.)

33. JACK-IN-THE-BOX (Grades 2-4)

A. Preparation and Materials: Draw a large Jack-In-The-Box on the board. On "Jack" write a number of letter combinations which the class has been studying.

B. Introduction to the Class: Let us name all the syllable endings which are printed on this Jack-In-The-Box before he goes back into his hiding place. (Children can name the sounds together, or one child can read at a time.)

Example:

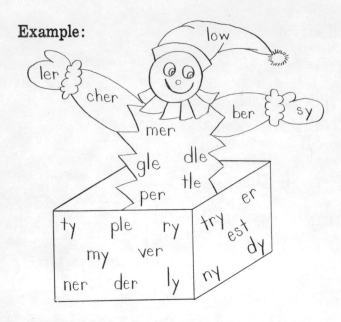

34. BEAT THE CLOCK (Grades 2-4)

A. Preparation and Materials: Cut a large clock of tagboard. Fasten a tagboard hand with a paper fastener so it will turn freely. Around the clock, write letters for the blend sounds.

Example:

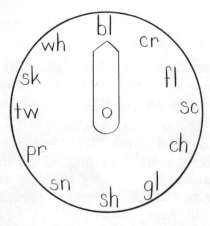

B. Introduction to the Class: I am going to call on one of you to be teacher for our game today. The teacher will turn the hand on this clock while the rest of you may name the sound of the letter to which the hand points.

C. Variation: The teacher may draw a large clock on the blackboard and have a child use a pointer as the class names the sounds of these initial blends.

35. HANG OUT THE WASH (Grades 2-3)

A. Preparation and Materials: Mimeograph sheets showing the illustration given below, and give one of these sheets to each child in the class. Children will need pencils.

Example:

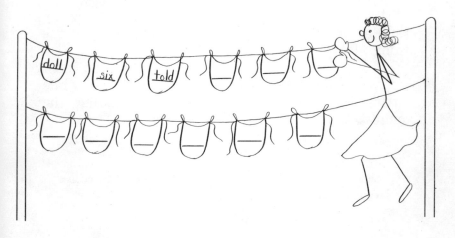

B. Introduction to the Class: As I call out each word, you may print the spelling of that word on one of the bibs which this girl is hanging out to dry. Start with the first bib in the top row, and write your answers on one bib after another. The teacher then pronounces such words as:

doll   six   told   bag   lip   miss   cat
ten   Tim   fur   muff   bib   back   buzz

C. Variation: For a quick classroom game, the diagram can be drawn on the board, and children called to write the letters for a variety of sounds on the bibs.

36. SIMON SAYS (Grades 2-8)

A. Preparation and Materials: None.

B. Introduction to the Class: Today we are going to play "Simon Says," but we're going to play it a little differently than usual. We shall all stand. I shall give you information, and if what I tell you is true, put your thumbs up. If what I tell you is false, put your thumbs down.

I shall try to fool you by sometimes putting my thumbs the wrong way. So listen carefully to the things I say so you won't be caught.

If I see your thumbs the wrong way, you must sit until the next game; but you can still play while sitting. Let's see who can remain standing the longest.

Sample Statements:

1. Simon says "n-e-s-s, ness" (spell the sound, then pronounce it) is a suffix. (Thumbs up)

2. Simon says "oi" is spelled "o-u." (Thumbs down)

3. Simon says "alligator" has 3 syllables. (Thumbs down)

4. Simon says "work" is the root word of "working." (Thumbs up)

5. Simon says short "i" says "ĭ." (Thumbs up)

- 136 -

37. I NAME IT — YOU PLACE IT (Grades 1-3)

A. Preparation and Materials: On the board, draw a diagram as given in the example below In each square, write the letters for a sound being studied in phonetic lessons.

Children will need drawing paper and beans, kernels of corn, or paper markers.

Children should fold their papers into squares, and fill in each square as shown on the board. (Lower grades would use fewer squares).

Example:

ay	ack	ill	e
old	ick	ub	oa
ight	ow	ing	oi
ig	et	op	ell

B. Introduction to the Class: Today we shall play, "I name it — you place it." Each of you has a paper folded into squares. The letter, or letters, for a sound is written in each square. You also have markers.

I shall say a sound. Look for the letter, or letters, for that sound on your paper. When you find it, place a marker on it.

(After the teacher has called all sounds, she should check for children who have not marked all the squares, and give them special help in the troublesome sounds.

(After all cards are filled, the children may remove the markers as the teacher calls each sound. Again she should check for children who have markers left after all sounds have been called, and give these children help. She can use the large chart on the board to aid in this special help.)

38. SPACE SHIP CRUISE (Grades 2-6)

A. Preparation and Materials: On the board, draw five space ships as pictured below. Write a number on each ship. This number tells the score a child receives if he chooses to board that particular ship.

Example:

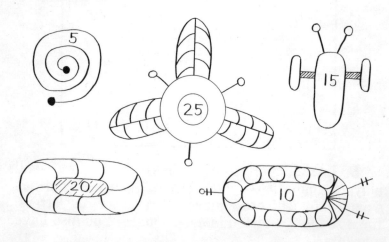

B. Introduction to the Class: Let's go on a space flight! Here are some ships we might use to travel in space.

You may choose whichever ship you wish; but before you can go, you must answer some questions.

The ships with lower numbers on them have easier questions. The ships with higher numbers have harder questions. The number on the ship also tells you how many points you win for answering the question.

We will go around the room, giving each child as many turns as possible in the playing time we have. At the end of our playing time the child with the most points wins a "trip to outer space." (Or, every child with 20 or more points may win the trip, or each child may be given a trip on the ship which carries the number corresponding with his total number of points.)

Sample Questions: (to be varied with grade level.)

5 Points — Name two sounds that "j" can make. Name the letter that is sometimes a vowel.

10 Points — Name three ways of writing the letters for the "A" sound. ("a" with "magical e," "ay," "ai.") Divide the word **cupboard** into syllables, and tell which rule this word follows.

15 Points — Spell the following words: (name five from spelling lesson). Name five words, each containing one of the five short vowel sounds.

20 Points — Define the following words: (name five from vocabulary list). Tell three rules for dividing words into syllables.

25 Points — Spell the following sounds: oi, ow, ight, ug, ip, ock. Spell and use in a sentence the following words: (name five from spelling lesson).

39. SAY IT — TAKE IT (Grade 2-6)

A. Preparation and Materials: Put a variety of objects on a table, the names of which contain sounds being studied by the class. For foundation-letter combinations the objects might be:

at — hat, bat	ox — box
ap — apple, cap, map	in — pin
an — fan, can, pan	ip — paper clip
et — letter	ut — button, nut
ar — toy car, star, jar	up — cup
en — pen, pencil	ot — bottle
op — top	

Divide the class into two teams.

B. Introduction to the Class: To begin our game, I shall call on a member of one team. He will come up to the table. I shall say a sound, "ut" for example. The child then has 30 seconds to find an object on the table the name of which has the "ut" sound in it. He might pick up the **nut.** (Teacher picks up the nut, writes **nut** on the board, and underlines the "ut" in **nut**) or the button. (Teacher demonstrates in the same manner.)

After he has found the object, he must repeat the sound I gave him, then name the object. He may then take the object to his seat. Then a member from the second team will come up, and I shall give him a new sound.

When all the objects on our table are gone, we shall see which team has the most objects. That team will be our winner.

C. Variation: Rather than saying the sounds, the teacher might hold up flash cards on which the sounds are written. In this way the child gets drill in recognizing the letter combinations on sight.

GAMES
SECTION 2
STRUCTURAL ANALYSIS

1. CAMERA (Grades 2-8)

A. Preparation and Materials: The teacher will need chalk and an eraser. Vary the difficulty of the vocabulary used to fit the level of your group.

B. Introduction to the Class: The game we are going to play now is called "Camera." All of you will shut your eyes while I write a word on the board. When I say "Click," you may open your eyes and "take a picture" of the word on the board. You will need to take your pictures very quickly, because I will erase the word as soon as you open your eyes. Then I will call on someone to "develop his film" and tell me the word that was written on the board.

(This game is devised to help children increase their speed in word recognition. It is particularly good as drill in easily confused words such as horse-house, when-then, was-saw, what-that, etc., for it demands instant appraisal of the structure of the entire word. It can also be used as a review of the new words presented for a particular day's reading lesson.)

2. QUIZ PANEL (Grades Kdg.-3)

A. Preparation and Materials: Arrange four chairs at the front of the room. Have a list of three or four-letter words to pronounce to the panel.

B. Introduction to the Class: These four chairs at the front of the room are for the members of our quiz panel. I shall pronounce a word for one panel member, and he must tell me a rhyming word.

For example, if I said **star,** he might say **car.** Then I will give the next panel member a new word.

When you miss, you may choose someone from the class to take your place on the panel.

C. Variations: This same activity can be used in a variety of ways. You might pronounce words to the panel members, and ask them to spell these words. Or give them a sound, and ask that they tell a word containing that sound. Or you might pronounce a sound, and ask that they tell a letter or a combination which could make that sound.

3. DIVIDING WORDS (Grades 2-3)

A. Preparation and Materials: None. You can name any common objects around the room or use words from the children's reading books.

B. Introduction to the Class: This week we have talked about dividing words (syllables), and the game we are going to play today will show me how well you can hear the parts of a word.

I shall say a word, and I should like you to hold up the number of fingers which tells how many parts are in that word.

For example, if I said **pencil**, how many fingers would you hold up, Connie? That's right, two. Can you hear the two parts in **pen-cil**, class? Now let's try some others.

(After children have become well-familiarized with common words, they will enjoy figuring out how many parts are in such words as **alligator, encyclopedia, hippopotamus, Constantinople,** etc.

(This game is devised strictly for ear training, and no words are written.)

4. MAKING NEW WORDS (Grades 1-3)

A. Preparation and Materials: Divide the board

into four sections. Number the sections 1 to 4. Provide chalk and an eraser in each section.

B. Introduction to the Class: To play our game today, we shall need four teams. Will you please number off by 4's? Will the 1's please sit in the front row (or go to whatever spot you designate), the 2's sit in the second row, etc? The number in each section of the board tells which team will use that space.

I shall call one member from each team to go to the board. Then I shall pronounce a word with "an" in it (or any letter combination the class is presently studying, such as "it," "at," "un," etc.). Listen carefully to the way the word begins. First write the letter or letters which would make that beginning sound. Finish each word with "an."

The first person to write correctly the word I pronounce will win a point for his team. At the end of the playing time the team with the most points wins.

(The teacher might then pronounce such words as **can, Dan, fan, man, pan, ran, tan, van,** etc.)

5. SYLLABIFICATION DRILL (Grades 2-8)

A. Preparation and Materials: Board space and chalk. Divide the class into two teams.

B. Introduction to the Class: One member from each team will go to the board. I shall pronounce a word. The children at the board will write the word, divide it into syllables, and write the number of the rule* which tells why the first syllable is divided as it is.

The first child to finish correctly will win a point for his team. Then a new child from each team will go to the board, and I shall pronounce a new word.

* See Appendix for detailed information on syllabification.

For example, if I said **topcoat,** you would write **top-coat (1).** (The teacher demonstrates this on the board, and answers any questions.)

Are there any further questions? Then we are ready to begin.

6. PREFIXES (Grades 3-8)

A. Preparation and Materials: Before using this drill game, the teacher should teach the meaning and usage of such common prefixes as:

re- again or back	in- into or not
com- with or together	un- not
dis- the opposite of	ex- out or from
pro- in front of	de- from
be- about, around, or all over	sub- under
en- in	pre- before

List several of these prefixes on the board. Opposite them, list words to which these prefixes can be added.

(Teams can be formed but are not necessary. This is a drill that can be used quickly during a regular class period.)

Example:

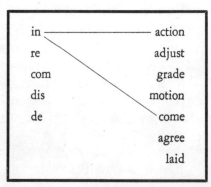

B. Introduction to the Class: I have made on the board a list of some of the prefixes we have studied. Opposite them are words with which they may be used.

I shall call on a child who will come to the front of the room. He will choose one prefix, and draw a line from it to a word with which it may be used. He will then pronounce the word and use it in a sentence.

If he answers correctly, he may choose the next child to answer. (Or, if teams are used, he will score a point for his team.)

C. Variation: Suffixes. The suffixes can be reviewed in a like manner. With the addition of a suffix, a word is often changed from one part of speech to another. The student should use in a sentence the word without the suffix, then with the suffix.

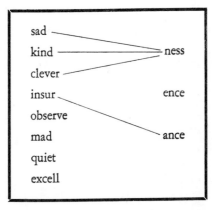

GAMES
SECTION 3
READING FOR MEANING

1. OUTGUESS THAT AUTHOR (Grades 1-8)

A. Preparation and Materials: The teacher may use any story book, preferably a short story, and definitely a story the class has not heard before.

B. Introduction to the Class: I am going to read a story to you now, but I will need your help. Once in a while I will stop in the middle of a sentence and ask you to guess what word comes next. I think you will be surprised to find out how well you can guess what word the author wrote next.

(At the close of this activity, it should be pointed out to the children that this is the technique of working out words by context clues. Children will find it useful in their individual reading, when they come to a word containing sounds they have not yet studied.

(This activity should be used sparingly, with a great overbalance of story time for the sheer joy of listening.)

2. DRAWING (Grades 2-3)

A. Preparation and Materials: Rule tagboard into 3" x 6" cards. Appoint a committee to cut the cards apart. Prepare about 30 cards.

On each card, write a noun which is capable. of illustration. A sample list of three-letter words is:

man	bug	sun	ten
six	tub	box	rat
bed	leg	pig	map
nut	pan	cup	jug
hen	pen	cap	pin
hat	fan	rug	dog
bag	bus	gun	cot
bat	lip	log	cat

Each child will need a sheet of drawing paper and crayons.

This game is devised for drill in reading speed, comprehension, and retention.

B. Introduction to the Class: I have some flash cards on which are written words we have studied. I will show you all the cards, one at a time. You will see each card for only a little while. (about 2 seconds).

After you have seen all the cards, I will say "Go." You may then take your crayons and paper and draw as many of the things as you can remember. I will give you 15 minutes to do your drawing.

Then we will look at the cards again. As we read each one together, you may put a red "x" beside the picture you drew for that word. Of course, if you forget to draw a picture for that word, you cannot put any "x" on your paper.

When we finish reading all the cards together, you may count your red "x's" to find out how many pictures you did correctly. The person with the most red "x's" will be our winner.

3. THE MOST IMPORTANT WORD (Grades 2-8)

This activity is designed to help children find the topic word in a sentence, or can be adapted to finding topic sentences in paragraphs. This skill is, of course, a necessary foundation before the ability of skimming can be developed.

When a story or sentences are written on the board, ask children to read each sentence and find the most important word in that sentence. Underline that topic word. Then erase all but these topic words. Ask children if they can look at one of these topic words and verbally reconstruct the sentence from which it came.

4. DEFINITIONS (Grades 2-8)

A. Preparation and Materials: Draw on the board a diagram similar to that shown below. In each square, write a word from the children's vocabulary list, varying the difficulty of the words given to fit the level of the group.

Children should fold drawing paper into a corresponding number of squares (fewer for lower grades) and write in the words shown on the board. Ask children to mix up the words as they write so that each word is in a different square from that shown on the board.

Children will need beans, kernels of corn, or paper for markers.

Example:

pillow	differ	season	nonsense
trail	promise	rate	conclude
rapid	disturb	offer	thirsty
moment	discover	allow	combine

B. Introduction to the Class: You have a word written in each square of your paper. I will give a definition. When you find the word that fits my definition, put a marker on it.

When you have marked four squares across, down, or vertically, say "Definitions!" Then we will check your card, and if you have marked each square correctly, you will be a winner. Then we will begin a new game.

Or, as more intensive drill, **all** definitions may be given. Then the teacher should look for children who have not marked all the squares, and give them help with the troublesome words.

(For additional review, the teacher can again call each definition, and children can remove the markers, one at a time, until the cards are clear again.)

C. Variations:

1. Arithmetic: Use the same idea, but in each square write a number, and then give children mental arithmetic problems to solve. Children may cover the number which answers each problem. Problems given could be addition, subtraction, multiplication, or division.

Example:

49	27	45	18
21	56	40	32
81	12	24	9
48	72	30	36

2. History, geography, science, civics, etc.: In each square, write an answer to a question on his-

tory (names, dates, places, etc.); geography (see example below). Children mark answers as the teacher asks questions.

Example:

Atlantic	S.A.	Canada	peninsula
North	Asia	Arctic	river
South	Pacific	Africa	Gulf
U.S.	Antarctic	Europe	England

5. SIGNAL (Grades 1-4)

A. Preparation and Materials: On strips of tagboard, write action directions, using vocabulary to suit the reading level of your group. Sample directions might be:

1. Write your last name on the board.
2. Put your left hand above your head.
3. Walk to the window and look outside.
4. Call "Here, Rover!" three times.
5. Jump up and down.
6. Skip to the door, then sit on the floor.

B. Introduction to the Class: On these cards are written directions. I will call a child's name as I hold up a card. If he can correctly do what the card tells, he may leave the reading circle, or get his coat for recess, etc.

- 155 -

6. ACTING

A. Preparation and Materials: Write a group of sentences on the board which show a variety of expressions.

Example:

> 1. "Do you like that game?"
> 2. "Susan! Come here right now!"
> 3. "That is my new bicycle."
> 4. "Help! Help! My house is on fire!"
> 5. "I am tired of working."

B. Introduction to the Class: I should like to see what good actors you can be. Several sentences are written on the board. Read each sentence to yourself. Think to yourself, "Is it asking a question? Does it sound exciting, sad, proud, or what?"

Decide how a person should feel if he were saying these sentences. I will call on some of you to see how well you can make your voices show the feeling of each sentence.

C. Variation: When children are reading aloud, ask them to be "good actors" and to let their voices portray the feelings expressed in the writing.

Let them practice reading aloud direct quotations, colorful descriptive passages, etc., with the true feelings intended by the author.

GAMES
SECTION 4
CREATIVE WRITING

1. THE GOOD FAIRY BOX (Grades 2-4)

A. Preparation and Materials: Cut a slot in the top of a shoe box. A committee may wish to cover and decorate the box. They may label it "The Good Fairy Box." Provide a supply of paper beside the box.

B. Introduction to the Class: I have noticed that many of you children have done very kind things for your classmates. Ann helped Jean to clean her desk today. John has lost his red crayon and Beth is sharing hers with him. (Cite several examples which have occurred in the classroom.)

Our new "Good Fairy Box" will let us tell those people how much we appreciate the kind things they do. Beside this box are slips of paper. When you see someone do a kind deed, you may take one of these slips of paper and write down what you saw him do. You may sign your notes "The Good Fairy," and put them through the slot in this box.

Each day someone may come up and read the notes in "The Good Fairy Box" to the class.

(This activity not only provides children with an opportunity for creative writing and experience reading, but also helps with self-discipline.)

2. "PASS IT ON" STORIES (Grades 3-8)

A. Preparation and Materials: Children will need pencils and writing paper. The teacher should list on the board a series of words which could be related in the sequence of a story, such as:

little boy . . . lost . . . woods . . . night
storm . . . old house . . . walk . . . home
or
space ship . . . moon . . . satellite . . . rocket
Mars . . . Venus . . . stars.

B. Introduction to the Class: I have listed on the board some words we could use to tell a story. Let's read these words together. (Children read the list together.)

What kind of a story do these words suggest to you, Sally? (Sally tells general idea of story that the words suggest to her.)

Does it suggest the same kind of story to you, Bill? (Bill might add a different "twist" to the plot.)

We are all going to begin writing a story, using as many of the words listed on the board as possible. At the end of two minutes I will say, "Pass it on." Then you will pass your paper to the child on your right. You will receive a paper from the child on the left. Read what he has written. Then begin writing on your new paper, adding to the story which the child before you has started.

You will pass your papers five times. At the end of that time you can each read aloud the story you are then holding.

3. ONE MINUTE STORIES (Grades 3-8)

A. Preparation and Materials: Have space available at the blackboard. Set out chalk and an eraser.

B. Introduction to the Class: Today we will play a ONE MINUTE STORY game. I will call a child to come to the board. He will begin writing a story.

After he has written one minute, I will ask him to stop — even if he is in the middle of a sentence. Then he may call another child to come to the board.

The second child will then continue the story until his minute is up. We will continue in this way until nine children have written. When the tenth child comes to the board, he will write a conclusion to the story. Then he may read the story aloud to the class.

You will need to watch the board carefully and be thinking what you might write if you were called on next.

4. ANSWERING QUESTIONS

A. Preparation and Materials: Play this game right after you have read an interesting adventure story to the children. They will need writing paper and pencils.

B. Introduction to the Class: We have all enjoyed this story so much, and now I wonder how well you remember what happened.

I am going to ask you several questions. Please write your answer to each question **in a complete sentence.** Use more than one sentence if you need it to fully explain your answer.

Sample Questions about **Peter Pan**

1. What strange and wonderful things could Nana, the dog, do for the children?
2. Why did Peter Pan come into Wendy's room?
3. Why did the Lost Boys live under the ground?
4. How could Captain Hook tell when the crocodile was near?
5. Why would Peter Pan not go back to live with Wendy?

GAMES
SECTION 5
MISCELLANEOUS

1. LIP READING (Grades 1-6)

A. Preparation and Materials: None.

B. Introduction to the Class: It is almost recess time now, and we are going to play a game to be excused from the room. I am going to make my mouth say a consonant sound, but I am not going to use any voice. Then I will call on someone. If he can tell me what sound he saw my mouth make, he may get his coat and line up quietly at the door.

2. CAN YOU FIND IT? (Grades 1-8)

A. Preparation and Materials: None. Use whatever is written on the board from a previous class period. Vary the difficulty of the questions to fit the level of your group.

B. Introduction to the Class: There are many sentences on the board which we used during our reading classes today. I am going to name some things that are on the board and see if you can find them. When you find the part I ask, you may erase it and line up quietly at the door for recess time.

Sample Questions:

1. Can you find a period?
2. Can you find a word that has "an" in it? (*Say* the sound rather than spell it.)
3. Can you find a little word inside a bigger word?
4. Can you find a word with three syllables?
5. Can you find a compound word?
6. Can you find a word with "ight" in it?
7. Can you find a capital letter?
8. Can you find a root word with an ending?

3. CODE MESSAGES (Grades 2-8)

A. Preparation and Materials: Write the letters of the alphabet on one section of the blackboard. Under each letter, write a number, beginning with 1 under "A," and ending with 26 under "Z."

On another section of the board write messages in code such as:

1. 20-15-4-1-25 9-19 6-18-9-4-1-25. (Today is Friday.)

2. 9-20 9-19 18-5-3-5-19-19 20-9-13-5. (It is recess time.)

Children will need writing paper and pencils.

B. Introduction to the Class: The game we are going to play today is just for fun. I have written the alphabet on one section of the board and under each letter I have written a number. Under "A" is the number 1, under "B" the number 2, and so on.

I have written some sentences using the code numbers instead of the letters on this other section of the board. Can you decode the message and find out what they say?

4. A - Z RELAY (Grades 1-2)

A. Preparation and Materials: Divide the blackboard into four sections. Number the sections from 1 to 4. Ten feet back from each section draw a chalk line on the floor. Provide each team with a piece of chalk.

B. Introduction to the Class: We will need four teams for our game today. Will you please count off by 4's? The number in each section of the board tells which team will use that space. On the floor is a chalk line behind which the first member of each team may stand. The teacher then calls one member from each team to stand on the chalk line;

facing the board. Will the other team members please line up behind your leader?

Example:

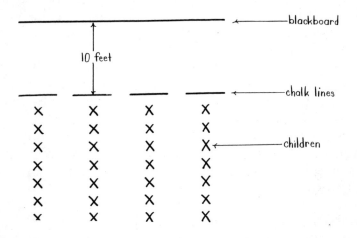

The first person on each team has a piece of chalk. He will walk up to the board, write "A," walk back, give the chalk to the next person on his team and go to the last place in the line. The second person will walk up and write "B," and so on. You will continue in this way until your team has written the entire alphabet through "Z." Each person on your team will have had several turns.

As soon as your team writes "Z" on the board, raise your hands so I will know you have finished. Then we will check the board. If your alphabet is written correctly, your team will win.

5. WRITE THE WORD (Grades 2-8)

A. Preparation and Materials: Each child will need a pencil and paper. The teacher will need a story book, using preferably a short story, and definitely one the children have not heard before.

Read the directions for "Outguess That Author"
(see GAMES, Section 2, Number 1, Page 151.)

B. Introduction to the Class: Do you remember
the game "Outguess That Author," which we played
together? This game is very similar, but instead
of **saying** the word you think will come next in the
story, I would like you to **write** it.

You will need your pencils and paper. I shall read
a story, and whenever I stop you will first think
what word could come next, and then write that
word. Please number each word as you go along.
The words must be spelled correctly to be counted
right. At the end of the story, we will correct our
papers together. The child with the most correct
answers will be our winner.

6. PENMANSHIP DRILL GAME (Grades 1-3)

A. Preparation and Materials: Children will
need writing paper and pencils.

B. Introduction to the Class: Today I am going
to tell you a story about NIXI, and as I tell you the
story you may "write a picture" about it.

"The Story of NIXI"

Once upon a time there was a little boy, just
your age, whose name was NIXI. NIXI was just
half a space tall, and one day he went for a walk.
You may draw NIXI walking across the first line
of your paper. (Teacher demonstrates on the
board.)

While NIXI was walking, he met a good friend
of his who was a soldier. The soldier was a full
space tall. You may draw the tall, straight soldier
walking along the next line of your paper. (Teacher
demonstrates on the board.)

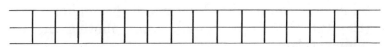

As NIXI and the tall soldier were walking along together it began to rain. The rain came down very fast. You may draw the rain on the next line of your paper. (Teacher demonstrates on the board.)

NIXI and the soldier did not want to get wet, so the soldier took NIXI to his tent to wait until the rain stopped. The soldier and NIXI had a very good time visiting in the soldier's tent. You may draw the tent on the next line of your paper. (Teacher demonstrates on the board.)

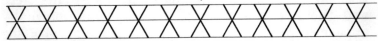

When the rain finally stopped, NIXI looked at his watch and noticed it was time to go home. The soldier had enjoyed his visit with NIXI so much that he gave him a nickel. You may draw the nickel on the next line of your paper. (Teacher demonstrates on the board.)

NIXI spent the nickel to buy a big rubber ball which he bounced all the way home. You may draw the ball on the next line of your paper. (Teacher demonstrates on the board.)

On the last line you may write NIXI's name. First make the big tall soldier, the rain, and another tall soldier. (Capital "N"). Then make another tall soldier. (Capital "I"). Now make the soldier's tent. (Capital "X"). Last of all, make another big tall soldier (Capital "I").

You may practice writing NIXI's name on the next line of your paper.

C. Variations: You may create other stories to afford further drill in whatever letters the children need practice. Children enjoy helping to create these new stories.

7. THE TREE (Grades 1-8)

A. Preparation and Materials: Draw a large tree on a sheet of tagboard. Cut small slits here and there where perhaps leaves would normally appear. Into each slip fasten a paper clip with the large loop towards the back. Tape the tree to the blackboard or tack it to the bulletin board.

Make small flash cards showing the current words being studied.

Example:

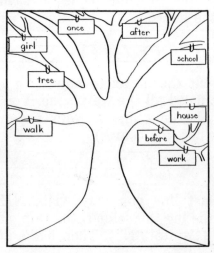

B. Introduction to the Class: I am going to hold up a card which shows one of our spelling words. I will show the card only a short time. Then I will call on someone to first say the word, spell it, and then use it in a sentence. If that person can do all three things, he may put the word on the tree.

C. Variations:

1. After all the words are on the tree, the teacher may reverse the process by pointing to a word, then covering it. A child may remove the card from the tree if he can say the word, spell it, and use it in a sentence.

2. Make flash cards showing addition, subtraction, multiplication, and division facts. Children must correctly solve the problem to place it on the tree.

3. Make flash cards showing letters or combinations of letters. Children must tell the sound to place a letter or letter combination on the tree.

8. TIC-TAC-TOE (Grades 3-8)

A. Preparation and Materials: Draw a tic-tac-toe game on the board. Divide the class into two teams.

B. Introduction to the Class: Today we are going to play tic-tac-toe. Team 1 will be the "X's" and team 2 will be the "O's."

One member from each team will go to the board. I will pronounce a spelling word for team 1. If that person correctly spells the word, he may put an X on the tic-tac-toe game. If he misses, he may **not** put an X, and a new member of his team will come to the board.

Then I will pronounce a new word for Team 2.

The team that first completes 3 X's or O's in a row will be our winner.

Example:

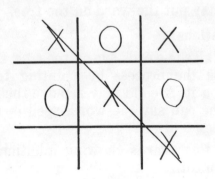

C. Variations:

1. For history or geography, ask appropriate questions, and those children answering correctly may mark in the tic-tac-toe game.

2. Marks in the squares can be made for correctly answering arithmetic problems.

3. Vocabulary drill can be given by pronouncing a word, and if a child can correctly define and use the word in a sentence, he earns a mark in the tic-tac-toe game.

9. QUICKIE PICK-UP (Grades 1-6)

A. Preparation and Materials: Children need reading books. This game is devised to liven up the oral reading period, to encourage children to recognize a complete sentence, and to give children more than one turn to read during the reading period. It should be used only after vocabulary has been reviewed and the lesson has been read silently.

B. Introduction to the Class: Today we are going to play a "Quickie Pick-up" game. I will begin reading our story. As I read, I will walk around the room. When I finish a sentence, I will tap a child on the head. That child will read the next sentence.

I will keep moving as the reading goes on, and as I tap each child he will read the sentence which is next.

C. Variation: This game can be varied by having a child start the reading, and the next child in the row continue as soon as the first child has completed a sentence. Then the child next in seating order quickly picks up when it is his turn.

10. READING BY PHRASE GROUPS

A. Preparation and Materials: Make a set of flash cards, each of which shows a group of words naturally phrased together when reading aloud.

Examples:

1. we are going
2. in the barn
3. heard them coming
4. all the way home
5. out to the road

B. Introduction to the Class: When we read aloud, we break a sentence into parts and read one complete part (or phrase) at a time. For example, we say:

"Mary went   into the house   to help Mother."

Saying the words in phrases like this helps us to read smoother and quicker.

I have some phrases on these flash cards. I shall hold up one card for just a short time. (About three seconds). Then I shall put it down and call on someone to tell me what the card said.

You will have to make your eyes see the whole phrase at once, so watch carefully!

INDEPENDENT WORK ACTIVITIES
SECTION 1
PHONETIC ANALYSIS

1. TOY BOX (Grades 2-4)

A. Preparation and Materials: Select toys or small articles, the names of which have been introduced in spelling or phonics class, and place them in a small cardboard box. Tape a written list of the contents to the bottom of the box.

Examples of what the box might contain are listed below.

1. Three-letter words

car	gun	jet	cap	fan	cup (plastic)
top	dog	pan	hat	box	map

2. Blend words

flag	clock	block	brush	plane
shoe	drum	wheel	spoon	train

3. "ar-or" words

fork	corn	cork	scarf	car
jar	yarn	star	barn	card

B. Introduction to the Class: I have put some toys in this box. The names of the toys are words we have been studying in our spelling class. If you would like to practice these words in your free time, you may take the box to your desk. Take out one toy at a time, and try to write its name. When the box is empty, turn it upside down. A list of the toys is written on the bottom of the box. You may check your spelling from this list.

2. PICTURE HOUSE (Grades 2-3)

A. Preparation and Materials: Cut two or more roof peaks along the top of a 9″ x 12″ sheet of tagboard. In each peak, write the letter or letters for a sound being currently studied in the phonics class. Cut a series of triangular slots in each house. (See example below).

Cut one 2″ square of tagboard for each slit. On

each square, draw a picture containing one of the sounds written on the roofs. Place these picture cards in an envelope and clip the envelopes to the picture house.

Example:

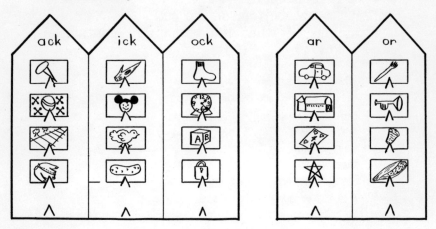

B. Introduction to the Class: I have put a new game on our free time table. It is called a picture house. On the roof of each house is the letter or combination of letters for a sound which we have studied. Below each roof are several slots.

In this envelope clipped to the house are many picture cards. Take out one picture at a time. Look at the picture and say its name to yourself.. The letter, or letters, for which you hear a sound, is written on the roof of one of the houses. Put the card in a slot below that roof.

Continue in this way until you have put each card in its proper house.

3. FLASH CARDS (Grades 1-8)

A. Preparation and Materials: Rule tagboard into 3″ x 6″ cards. Appoint a committee to cut the cards. On each card, write a key word for a sound being studied in the phonics class. Add new cards as new units are studied. Put a rubber band around the complete set.

B. Introduction to the Class: These flash cards contain the key words for the sounds we have been studying. One of you may hold up the cards, one at a time, while your friend reads the words.

I will be adding new cards each time we study new sounds, so you will want to use these flash cards often to see how well you can remember the new sounds.

4. MATCHING (Grades 1-3)

A. Preparation and Materials: Draw two columns of pictures on 9″ x 12″ sheets of tagboard. For each picture in the first column, draw in the second column a picture beginning with the same sound.

Punch a hole by each picture. Fasten shoe laces in the holes by the pictures in the first column.

Example:

B. Introduction to the Class: On this sheet of tagboard are two columns of pictures. A shoestring is fastened by each picture in the first column. There is a hole by each picture in the second column.

Say the name of the first picture in the first column. Listen to the way it begins. Then find a picture in the second column the name of which begins the same way. Use the shoestring to match the pictures which begin with the same sound. (The teacher should demonstrate threading the shoelace to match the two pictures which begin with the same sound.)

5. HOPSCOTCH (Grades 2-4)

A. Preparation and Materials: Rule 9″ x 12″ tagboard into 12 squares. Draw a picture containing the letter (or letters) for a sound studied by the class in each square. Label each picture omitting the letter (or letters) for the stressed sound.

Under each omitted letter (or letters) for a sound cut a small triangular slot (see example below).

Make a small card showing the letter (or letters) for each of the omitted sounds. Put these cards in an envelope, and clip the envelope to the hopscotch card.

Example:

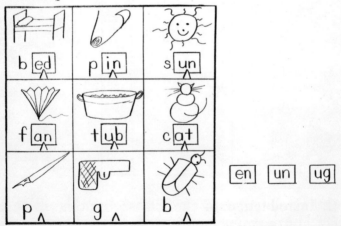

B. Introduction to the Class: Do you remember

the hopscotch game we played all together? (See GAMES, Section 1, Number 5, Page 105.) I have made a hopscotch game which you can play all by yourselves in your free time.

There is a picture in each square of this card. Under each picture is written **part** of the name of that picture, but part of the word is missing. Say the word to yourself. Look at the letters already written and decide what letter is missing.

Then find that letter on one of the little cards in the envelope attached to the hopscotch game. Fit the letter card in the slot like this (teacher demonstrates) so the complete word will then be written.

Then go on to the next square and do the same thing. See if you can "hop" all the squares.

6. SOUND PUZZLES (Grades 2-4)

A. Preparation and Materials: Rule 9″ x 12″ tagboard into 12 squares. In each square illustrate one of the phonetic sounds the class has studied.

Example:

Cut small tagboard cards, and on each card write the letter of a sound heard in one of the illustrations.

Put these cards in an envelope and attach the envelope to the illustrated sheet.

B. Introduction to the Class: This card is divided into squares, and in each square is a picture. Attached to the picture sheet is an envelope containing one letter card for each picture. Lay the picture sheet on your desk, and beside it place the small letter cards.

Now look at the first picture. It is a boy. Which of the sounds written on the cards do you hear in the word "boy," Karen? That's right, "oy." Put the card that says "oy" on top of the picture of the boy. Then match the other pictures and letters in the same way.

7. REFERENCE BOOK (GROUP) (Grades 1-3)

A. Preparation and Materials: Cut large tagboard sheets in half and store a quantity of these. They will then be ready for use as needed. Supply two or three ring clips, or any other fastening device that will allow the pages of the reference book to be opened flat.

Sample Reference Book Pages:

B. Introduction to the Class: As we study each unit in our phonics class, I would like to ask a committee to make a page for our large class reference book. Each page will show the letters for the sounds in the unit we are studying, and will have pictures to illustrate each sound. We will fasten all the pages together with rings.

Whenever we wish to review the sounds we have studied, we can stand our book up on the chalk tray and turn to the page we need. Each page will be large enough so that all of us can see it at once.

If you are asked to be on the committee to make one of these pages, you will first need to make a list of the letters for the sounds in the unit we are studying. Then your committee members can get together in your free time and decide what picture you will use to illustrate each sound.

Then bring your list to me, and after I have checked it, I will give you a large sheet of tagboard to use for your page. When you have finished your page, I will help you fasten it in the book.

8. PHONICS TV (Grades 1-8)

A. Preparation and Materials: Cut a large hole in the side of a big cardboard box, leaving a 2″ margin at the top and two sides, and a 6″ margin at the bottom. Cut two small circles on each side of the box and insert lengths of broom handle. (See example below).

Provide paint, two small dowel rods (for antennae), and a lump of clay.

You will need a roll of wrapping paper. After the broom handles have been mounted in the TV set, tack one end of the roll to each handle.

The phonics pages can be stapled, one above the other, on the wrapping paper roll. See the illustration in the preceding activity for a sample of the content of each of these individual pages.

As the handles are rolled, succeeding pages of phonics materials can be viewed.

Example:

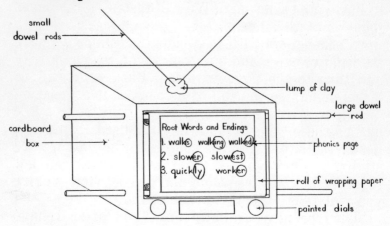

B. Introduction to the Class: I would like to have a committee help make a TV set. I have cut a hole for a screen in the sides of this cardboard box. The committee may paint the box, put on dials, and use these dowel rods and this lump of clay to make "rabbit ears" antennae as in this picture. (The teacher shows children the illustration above.)

Another committee can work on pages to show the letters for the sounds we have been studying in our phonics lessons. (See "Sample Reference Book Pages" in the preceding activity.)

I will help you mount these pages on the roll of wrapping paper that will be fastened inside the TV set. Then as you turn the handles you can watch our phonics TV. You can look at this TV in your free time, or we can use it together when we wish to review our phonics work.

C. Variations: Children might enjoy making

other TV sets to display creative stories, trip logs, a class diary, phonics, poems, material from a social studies unit, etc.

9. FLANNEL BOARD ACTIVITIES

To make a flannel board, cover a 24″ square (or larger) sheet of Cellotex (brand name) with flannel. The flannel board can be hung on a wall within children's reach, or rested on the chalk tray.

Paste small scraps of flannel or sandpaper to the back of each picture or card to be displayed, and it will stick to the flannel board.

Among the phonetic drill activities which can be carried out with a flannel board are:

A. MATCHING WORDS THAT BEGIN ALIKE (Grades 1-2)

1. Preparation and Materials: Cut tagboard into 4″ squares. Illustrate objects which begin with double consonants, making two pictures beginning with each sound. Paste scraps of flannel or sandpaper on the back of each card. Put all the cards in an envelope.

Example:

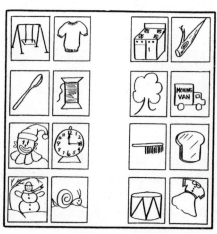

2. Introduction to the Class: We have been studying blend words, and the pictures in this envelope show words which begin with blend sounds. There are two pictures which begin with each blend sound. Place the cards which begin alike side by side on the flannel board.

B. YES OR NO (Grades 1-2)

1. Preparation and Materials: Cut thirteen 4" squares of tagboard, and twelve that are 2" x 4". Use one larger card to make the stressed sound cards (in red letters), and the rest to make the pictures. Make six pictures that begin with the stressed sound, and six that do not. Use the 2" x 4" cards to make six "yes" and six "no" labels for the pictures. Paste scraps of flannel or sandpaper to the back of each card. Put all the cards in an envelope.

Example:

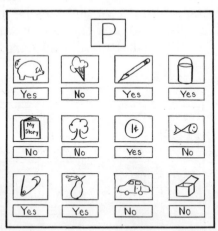

2. Introduction to the Class: You will find in this envelope a card with the letter "P" (or the symbol for whatever the stressed sound might be) written on it in red. Put that card at the top of the flannel board. Next take out all the picture cards and place them in rows on the board. Next you will find many cards which say either "yes" or "no."

Look at the first picture. Say its name to yourself. If it begins with the sound of "P," put a card that says "yes" under that picture. If you do not hear the sound of "P" at the beginning of that word, put a card that says "no" under it. Then go on and do the same with each of the other pictures.

C. MATCHING BEGINNING SOUNDS

1. Preparation and Materials: Cut twenty-five 4-inch squares of tagboard. On five of these cards, write five different sounds currently being studied by the class. Use the remaining cards to make four pictures which begin with the same sound as each lettered card. Paste scraps of flannel or sandpaper to the back of each card. Place all these cards in an envelope.

Example:

2. Introduction to the Class: In this envelope you will find cards showing the letters for five of the sounds we are studying. Place these cards, one above the other, along the left-hand side of the flannel board. (The teacher demonstrates.)

Then take out the pictures in the envelope. Look at one picture at a time. Listen to the way its name begins. Put it in the row with the card which tells how that word begins. There will be four pictures for each sound.

10. MATCHING RHYMING WORDS
(Grades Kdg.-3)

A. Preparation and Materials: Rule two sheets of 9" x 12" tagboard into nine squares each. Draw a picture in each square of the first sheet.

For each picture on the first sheet draw a rhyming picture on the second sheet. Cut the pictures on this second sheet into separate cards. Put the cards in an envelope, and clip it to the first sheet.

Example:

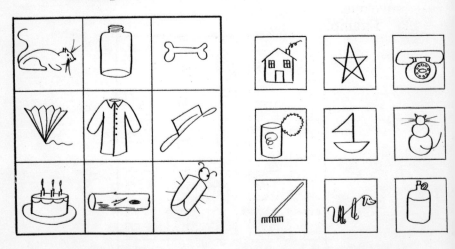

B. Introduction to the Class: On this large sheet are nine pictures. In the attached envelope are nine separate picture cards. Each picture card rhymes with one of the pictures on the large sheet.

Let's look at the first picture card. It shows a house. Now look at the pictures on the big sheet. With which picture does it rhyme, Joan? That's right, the mouse. So I will put the picture of the house on top of the picture of the mouse. Say the words **mouse** and **house.** Can you hear them rhyme?

Now we can take the next picture card and find where it belongs on the large sheet. We will work in this same way until all the rhyming pictures are matched.

11. SOUND DISCS (Grades 2-3)

A. Preparation and Materials: Cut one tagboard circle 5″ in diameter, and another 7″ in diameter. Place these circles, one on top of the other, center together, and fasten them through the center with a paper fastener so they will turn freely.

On the inner disc, write a word foundation letter combination. On the outer disc, write initial consonants which can be prefixed to the center letters to form new words.

Example:

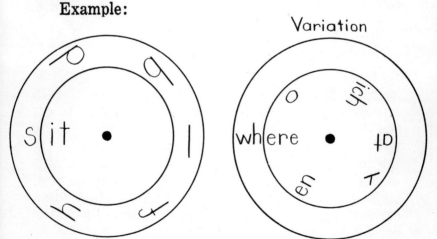

Variation

B. Introduction to the Class: We have talked together about how words can be changed to new words by changing the first letters. You may use these sound discs in your free time to practice these changes.

First look at the letters for a sound which are written on the inner disc. Say that sound to yourself. Then turn the outer disc so that one of the outside letters will come before the letters for the sound written on the inner disc. For example, this disc says "it" in the center, and I have turned the outer disc so the "s" is in front of "it." (The teacher demonstrates.) What word does that make, class? Yes, "sit." Now I put the letter "h" in front of "it." What is the new word now, class? Yes, "hit."

You may practice in the same way in your free time. See if you can read all the new words you make by adding a new beginning letter to the sound, the letters for which are written on the inner disc.

C. Variations:

1. Sound Strips: Cut two tagboard strips, 2″ x 5″ each. On one strip write the letter or letters for an initial consonant or blend sound, and after it cut two horizontal slits 2″ long. On the second strip, write your familiar endings which will blend with the initial consonant to form new words. Slip this second strip through the horizontal slits in the first strip, as illustrated below. By sliding the ending card through the slits, children can blend the initial consonant with each new ending to form new words.

Example:

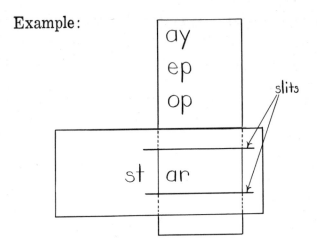

2. Sound Pop-ups: Write a familiar word on a 6″ x 4″ strip of tagboard. Cut about six 3″ x 4″ cards, and on each write an initial consonant. Fasten them to the larger card as illustrated below so that each card can swing up. Children swing up one card at a time and read the new words formed by changing the initial consonant.

Example:

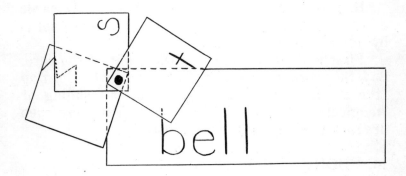

12. WORD CARDS WITH ENDINGS OR "MAGICAL e" (Grades 2-6)

A. Preparation and Materials: On the front of a flash card, write a root word (or a word that can be changed by adding "magical e") and on the back, write an ending (or "magical e"). When the card is folded properly (see example), the ending should touch the root word.

Example:

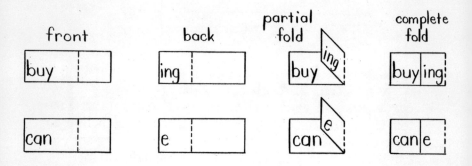

B. Introduction to the Class: These new cards on the free time table will help you make new words by adding endings or "magical e."

First look at the word on the front of the card. Say the word to yourself. Then fold over the flap (the teacher demonstrates) so that an ending or "magical e" is added to the word. You may then practice reading these new words.

13. PHONICS PRACTICE

A. Preparation and Materials: Write on the blackboard a list of the letters for the sounds being

currently studied in the phonics class.
Set out chalk and an eraser.

B. Introduction to the Class: Some of you may wish to use your free time to practice using the new sounds we are learning. The letters for our new sounds are listed on the board. You may write after each sound as many words as you can think of which contain this sound.

Example:

1. un — bun, bunny, fun, funny, gun, run, sun

2. ig — big, dig, pig

3. it — bit, fit, hit, kit, kitten, lit, little, mitten, pit, sit

4. ap — apple, cap, rap, tap, map, happy

5. ug — bug, dug, rug, tug

6. ot — hot, not, pot, rot

INDEPENDENT WORK ACTIVITY
SECTION 2
STRUCTURAL ANALYSIS

1. SYLLABLES (Grades 2-6)

A. Preparation and Materials: Rule tagboard into 3″ x 6″ cards. Ask a committee to cut the cards. Write a word from the children's reading vocabulary on the front of each card. On the back, write the number which tells how many syllables are in that word. Put a rubbber band around the complete set.

B. Introduction to the Class: On each of these flash cards I have written a word. On the back of each card is the number which tells how many syllables are in that word.

This card says "Grandmother." (The teacher holds up the card.) How many syllables are in that word, Jack? Yes, there are three syllables. Now I will let you see the back of the card. The teacher turns the card over.) The number "3" is written on the back.

Two of you together may play a game with these cards One of you may hold up a card with the word facing your partner. First he will tell you the word, and then he will tell you how many syllables that word has.

Then you may turn the card over to show him the number on the back. That number will tell him if his answer is correct.

2. DIVIDING WORDS (Grades 2-6)

A. Preparation and Materials: Use any flash cards which the class is currently using. Under the rubber band encircling the cards, insert an envelope containing about fifty ¼″ x 3″ strips of colored tagboard.

B. Introduction to the Class: I have put something new in the group of flash cards on our free time table. It is an envelope containing many narrow strips of colored paper.

We have talked about dividing words, and have studied several rules to help us in dividing words.* Let's review those rules together. (The teacher helps the class review rules for dividing words.)

You can practice dividing words with our regular flash cards and these new strips of colored paper. First read the word on the flash card to yourself. Then think how many parts that word has. Lay the flashcard on your desk. Put a colored strip of paper between the letters to show where the word divides. (The teacher should demonstrate this to the class.)

Example:

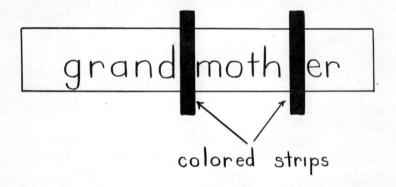

colored strips

3. COMPOUND WORDS (Flannel Board Activity) (Grades 2-3)

A. Preparation and Materials: (To make a flannel board see the instructions given in INDEPENDENT WORK ACTIVITIES, Section 1, Activity 9, Page 185.) Cut twenty 4" squares of tagboard. Use these to make pairs of cards, one illustrating each

---

* See Appendix for detailed information on teaching Syllabification.

part of a compound word. Paste flannel or sand-paper to the back of each card. Put all the cards in an envelope.

Example:

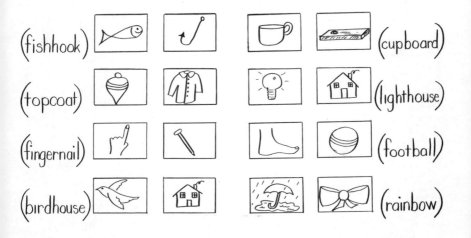

B. Introduction to the Class: In this envelope you will find many picture cards. Among them you will find pairs which go together to form compound words. Place each pair of pictures side by side on the flannel board to show the compound words you have found.

C. Variation: Rather than using illustrations, write the words themselves on the cards. Children would then match pairs of words which form compound words.

4. ROOT WORDS AND ENDINGS (Grades 2-3)

A. Preparation and Materials: Cut pairs of tag-board strips 2" x 6". On one strip, write a root word. After it, cut two horizontal slits $2\frac{1}{4}$" long.

On the second strip, write endings which could be added to the root word. Insert the second strip through the slits in the first strip.

Example:

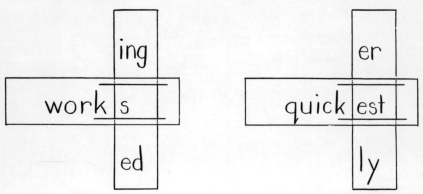

B. Introduction to the Class: We have been studying root words and endings, and you may practice using them with these cards. First read the root word. Then slide the card with the endings, and practice reading the new words formed each time you change the ending. (The teacher should demonstrate this.)

C. Variation: One ending can be used with a variety of root words by making the cards like this:

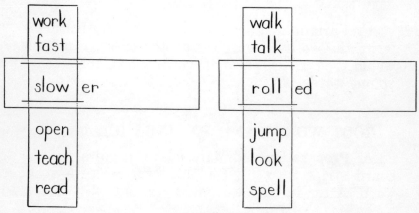

INDEPENDENT WORK ACTIVITIES
SECTION 3
READING FOR MEANING

1. PICTURE STORIES (Grades 1-2)

A. Preparation and Materials: Write a story on a 9″ x 12″ sheet of tagboard. Omit some words which are in the children's reading vocabulary. Draw a picture "clue" for each omitted word. Under each picture cut a small triangular slot. (See example below.)

Make 1″ x 2″ cards showing the missing words. Put these cards in an envelope and clip the envelope to the tagboard story sheet.

Example:

B. Introduction to the Class: Boys and girls, there is a story written on this card. But some of the words of the story are missing. There is a picture "clue" to help you know what word should fit there. The envelope attached to this card contains all the missing words.

First take the word cards out of the envelope, and lay them face up on your desk. Next start reading the story. Each time you come to a missing word, find the card which says that word. The picture will help you. Fit each word into the slot where it belongs, like this. (The teacher demonstrates.) After you have fitted each word card into its proper slot, you will enjoy reading the story over again to yourself.

C. Variation: As a more advanced seatwork activity, write a story on the board omitting some words and inserting picture "clues" as in the example above. Children are to copy the story, writing in the missing words. They may draw the picture clues above the added words if time allows.

2. SENTENCE PUZZLES (Grades 2-4)

A. Preparation and Materials: Write sentences, each containing several phrases, on strips of tagboard. Cut each sentence into its phrase parts. Put the phrases for each complete sentence into a small envelope, and put all the small envelopes into a larger envelope. Vary the vocabulary and difficulty of sentence structure to fit the needs of your group.

Example:

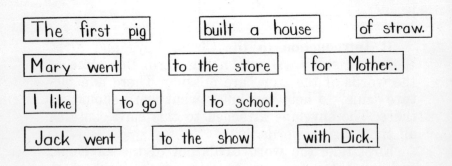

B. Introduction to the Class: I have put several envelopes into this large envelope. Each small envelope contains several phrases which you can put together to form a complete sentence.

Let's look inside one of the small envelopes. One of the cards says, "built a house." (The teacher shows each phrase card to the class as she reads it.) Another says, "of straw." The last card says, "The first pig." Do you think you could arrange these cards to make a complete sentence, George?

Very good, George! Your sentence says, "The first pig built a house of straw."

In your free time some of you may wish to take this envelope to your desk. Open one of the small envelopes at a time and arrange the phrase cards to make a complete sentence. Then open the next envelope and do the same thing. If you have trouble, perhaps Tommy or Susan (fast readers) would help you.

When you put this game away, be very careful to put just the phrases from one complete sentence into each envelope. Then it will be easier for the next person who uses them.

(From time to time you might ask a faster reader to look through the envelopes and straighten out any misplaced phrases, or to replace any that are missing. This, of course, requires an added degree of skill.)

3. JIGSAW PUZZLE (Grades 1-3)

A. Preparation and Materials: Mount a colorful picture and a short story or poem about that picture on heavy tagboard. Cut this to make a jigsaw puzzle. Put the pieces in an envelope.

An old Mother Goose book with one rhyme per page is very good to use. In this way an entire page can be mounted at one time, for it contains both the picture and the story.

As an additional free-time activity, children may enjoy writing their own stories which they can mount and cut to make new puzzles for the class.

B. Introduction to the Class: I have put the pieces of a jigsaw puzzle in this envelope. You may put it together in your free time. When you are finished, the puzzle will show a picture and a story about that picture. I think you will enjoy reading the interesting story you find!

4. CLASSROOM HELPERS (Grades 2-6)

A. Preparation and Materials: Ask a committee to cut a slot in the top of a shoe box, decorate the box, and label it, "Classroom Helpers." Write classroom housekeeping duties on slips of paper and put these slips in the "Classroom Helpers" box.

Sample Duties:

1. Please ask a boy or girl who has his work done to help you wash the blackboards.
2. Please feed our goldfish.
3. Please look in each desk to see if it is clean. If you see a desk that is not clean, ask the boy or girl to clean it when his work is done.
4. Please dust the window sills.
5. Please pick up the scraps of paper you see on the floor.

B. Introduction to the Class: If you finish your work early today, and would like to help in making our room look nice, you may take a slip from this "Classroom Helpers" box. Each slip tells of a classroom job which needs doing. You may read the slip and do whatever it says.

5. FLANNEL BOARD ACTIVITIES

(To make a flannel board see the instructions given in INDEPENDENT WORK ACTIVITIES, Section 1, Activity 9, Page 185.)

A. MATCHING PICTURES AND TITLES
(Grades 1-2)

1. Preparation and Materials: Cut eleven 4" squares of tagboard. On one, write in red the letter for the stressed sound. On the other ten cards, illustrate words containing this sound.

Cut ten 2" x 4" strips of tagboard. Use these to make a written label for each of the illustrations.

Paste scraps of flannel or sandpaper to the back of each card. Put all these cards in an envelope, and label it with the letters for the stressed sound.

Example:

2. Introduction to the Class: In this envelope are many pictures. On separate cards are the names of these pictures. There is also one card with the letters "le" (or the letters for whatever stressed sound may be) in red letters. All the pictures and words in this envelope contain the "le" sound.

First take the card written in red letters, the "le" card. Put it at the top of the flannel board. Next take all the pictures and put them in rows on the board. Then take one word card at a time, and put it under the picture it names.

When you finish, say the sound of the letters shown at the top of the board. Then read each of the words you have placed under the pictures. Listen for the "le" sound in each word.

B. MAKING SENTENCES (Grades 2-3)

1. Preparation and Materials: Write sentences on tagboard. Cut the words apart, and paste scraps of flannel or sandpaper to the back of each card. Put the words of each sentence into a small envelope and put all these smaller envelopes into a larger envelope.

Example:

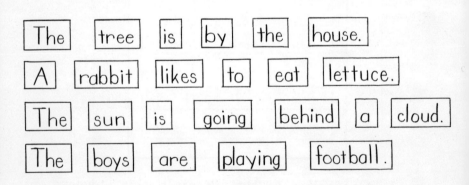

2. Introduction to the Class: In this large envelope you will find several smaller envelopes. In each of these small envelopes are several words which can be put together and make a complete sentence. Open one small envelope at a time. Arrange the words on the flannel board to make a sentence. Then open the other envelopes, one at a time, and do the same thing.

When you put the game away, you will need to be very careful to put the right words in each envelope. (Faster children can, from time to time, check the envelopes to straighten out misplaced cards, or to replace missing ones. This requires an added degree of skill.)

C. MATCHING PICTURES AND STORIES
(Grades 1-2)

1. Preparation and Materials: Mount interesting pictures on squares of tagboard. Write a sentence or short story (children could help in composing them) about each picture on separate strips of tagboard. Paste scraps of flannel or sandpaper on the back of each of these cards. Put all the cards in an envelope.

Example:

2. Introduction to the Class: In this envelope you will find several pictures, and several short stories about these pictures. First place all the pictures on the flannel board. Then place each story under the picture about which it tells.

6. DEFINITIONS (Grades 2-8)

A. Preparation and Materials: Rule tagboard into ten 2″ x 3″ cards. On each card, write one word from the children's vocabulary list. Use black ink.

Make a corresponding number of tagboard cards 2″ x 6″. Using red ink, write a definition for one of the above words on each card.

Example:

planet	A heavenly body which orbits the sun.
sun	A flaming ball of gaseous matter.
moon	A heavenly body which orbits a planet.
star	A faraway sun.

B. Introduction to the Class: I would like to see how well you know the meaning of words. In this envelope you will find ten cards with words written in black ink. Put these cards one above another along the left-hand side of your desk. Then read the definition on the first red card. Find the black card which fits the definition, and place the two cards side by side. Match all the words and their definitions in the same manner.

C. Variation: As a related seatwork activity for grades 4-8, make a list of appropriate words on the board. Children may write a definition of each word. To correct papers, ask one child to read the dictionary definitions to the class so that each child may evaluate his work.

7. OPPOSITES (Grades 1-2)

A. Preparation and Materials: Cut twenty 3″ x 6″ cards of tagboard. Use these to make ten pairs of opposite words, such as: **hot, cold; big, little; up, down;** etc. Put one card from each pair in a row, one above the other, along the left-hand side of a Plymouth Chart (brand name). Put the remaining cards along the bottom pocket of the chart.

Example:

prepared for use					in use		
hot					hot		cold
big					big		little
up					up		down
on					on		off
short					short		tall
fat					fat		thin
night					night		day
dry					dry		wet
day	wet	thin	tall				
down	cold	little	off				

B. Introduction to the Class: We have discussed the meaning of the word "opposite." Can you tell me two words which have opposite meanings, Jim? Yes, **on** and **off**.

I have put some flash cards on the left side of this chart. At the bottom of the chart are cards showing words with opposite meaning. The first word along the left side of the chart is **hot**. Can you find a card in the bottom row which has the opposite meaning of **hot**, Susan? Yes, cold. Will you put that card on the chart beside the word **hot**?

In your free time you may match the other opposite words in the same way.

8. CUT-APART STORIES (Grades 1-3)

A. Preparation and Materials: Mount an interesting action or mood picture on tagboard or heavy construction paper. Discuss the picture with the class. Have them compose a short story about the picture. As they dictate, write the story on tagboard, making sure the story contains at least four lines.

Hold up this story card, and ask several children to read the story aloud to the class. Then cut the lines of the story apart, and put these separate lines in an envelope. Fasten the envelope to the back of the picture card.

Example:

> The mother butterfly
>
> lays her eggs on a leaf.
>
> Caterpillars come out of
>
> the eggs. Soon the caterpillars
>
> spin cocoons. A Butterfly
>
> comes out of each cocoon.

B. Introduction to the Class: Today you helped write a story about this picture. After I wrote your story, I cut each line apart. I have put the parts of the story in this envelope which is fastened to the back of the picture.

In your free time you may take this picture and envelope to your desk. Arrange all the parts of the story face up on your desk. Then see if you can put them in proper order so that you may read the story again.

INDEPENDENT WORK ACTIVITIES
SECTION 4
CREATIVE WRITING

1. PICTURE DICTIONARIES (Grades 1-3)

A. Preparation and Materials: Place several commercial picture dictionaries on the free time table.

B. Introduction to the Class: I have placed several picture dictionaries on the phonics table. Let's look at one to see how we might use it.

You will see there are many pictures in this book. Beside each picture is the written word for whatever is shown in the picture. At the beginning of the book are words beginning with "A." Next come words beginning with "B," and so on. The words are all in alphabetical order. The big letter at the top of each page tells how all the words on that page will begin.

When you would like to know how to spell a word, first say the word to yourself. Listen to the first sound of the word. Decide what the first letter of that word would be.

Next open the dictionary to the section on that letter. Look at the pictures until you find the one you want. Look beside the picture and you will find the word you wanted to spell.

You will find a dictionary very useful when you want to write stories, letters, etc., in your free time.

2. WRITING STORIES (Grades 2-8)

A. Preparation and Materials: Clip an interesting action or mood picture from a magazine. Mount the picture on a colorful backing sheet. Pin the picture to the bulletin board.

B. Introduction to the Class: I found this interesting picture in a magazine and thought you would enjoy looking at it. What do you see in the picture, Don? What is happening? How does it make you feel? Does it remind you of something you have done? (Ask whatever motivating questions are appropriate to arouse interest in that particular picture.)

I will pin this picture on the bulletin board. In your free time you might wish to write a short story about the picture. You may pin your stories around the picture so that all of us can read and enjoy them.

3. DAILY CLASS NEWSPAPER ON BOARD (Grades 1-8)

A. Preparation and Materials: Reserve one section of the blackboard, and have chalk and an eraser set out. Children will need pencils and scrap paper.

B. Introduction to the Class: Many of you have news you want to share with your classmates each day. If you have news you know the class would find interesting, write it on a scrap of paper. Bring that paper to me, and after I have corrected it, you may write your news on this section of the board. After everyone who wishes has contributed his news, we will read our classroom newspaper out loud.

4. STORIES FOR SHUT-INS (Grades 2-4)

Children enjoy using their free time to write cheerful stories with colorful illustrations. These stories and pictures can be fastened together to make a booklet. The booklet could then be sent to a sick classmate, a local hospital, a home for the aged, etc.

5. UNIT STUDY COMMITTEE (Grades 3-8)

Committees can be chosen to gather additional

information for a unit under study by the class. These committees can use their free time to read for information, and then write up their findings.

After the teacher has corrected their written work, they can put the information on large charts to be used as a reference source by the class.

6. CLASS RULES (Grades 3-8)

If the class is planning a field trip or party, a committee can be chosen to formulate rules of behavior for the class. The committee can use their free time to discuss, formulate, and write these rules.

The committee can then present their suggestions to the class for discussion and final decisions.

The teacher can check the committee's written report, and the children can then write the rules on a chart for class review before the special event takes place.

7. ESSAY CONTEST (Grades 2-8)

From time to time topics can be presented to the class for essay contests. Children can write essays on this topic in their free time, and give them to classmates who have been selected as judges.

After all those who wish have entered their essays, the judges may select first, second, and third place winners.

Class time can be taken for all essays to be read aloud, and for the judges to announce the winners.

All essays can then be displayed on the bulletin board. Perhaps the judges would enjoy making "ribbons" to be displayed with the winning essays.

Sample topics:

1. EARLY GRADES
   A. Spring
   B. When I grow up, I want to be _____.
   C. I like my school because _____.
   D. My Family
   E. What I Like About Christmas.
2. LATER GRADES
   A. The country I would most like to visit is_____.
   B. Democracy
   C. A Famous Man in History
   D. Why I Enjoy Art
   E. My Hobby

Some class time should be taken to discuss the criteria for a good essay: originality of thought, good grammar and sentence construction, neatness, etc.

8. SCHOOL OR CLASS NEWSPAPER
(Grades 1-8)

Children can collect room or school news to be written, duplicated, and distributed throughout the class or school. Room activities, new students, units of study, creative writing (prose or poetry) are among the types possible. This activity can be adapted to any grade level. Children can edit and illustrate the paper. "Reporters" can volunteer for assignments which they complete in their free time.

INDEPENDENT WORK ACTIVITIES
SECTION 5
MISCELLANEOUS

1. ALPHABET CARDS (Grades 1-2)

A. Preparation and Materials: Rule tagboard into twenty-six 3″ squares. Ask a committee to cut these squares, and to write one letter of the alphabet on each card. Put a rubber band around the complete set.

B. Introduction to the Class: I have placed a set of alphabet cards on the free-time table. You may use these cards in several different ways.

1. You may stand them up along the chalk tray of the blackboard in alphabetical order.

2. You may stand them up along the chalk tray of the blackboard, and see how many words you can make using just these letters.

3. Two of you may work together. One may hold up a card and ask the other to name a word that begins with that letter.

4. Two of you may work together. One may hold up a card and ask the other to tell what sound that letter makes.

2. ANAGRAMS (Grades 2-4)

A. Preparation and Material: Rule tagboard into 104 1-inch squares. Ask a committee to cut the squares and to write one letter of the alphabet on each card. They can make four complete alphabet sets.
Put these cards in a small box.

B. Introduction to the Class: In this box are many little cards, and on each card is a letter of the alphabet. Four of you together may play a game with these cards in your free time.
First lay all the cards face down in the center

of the table. Each player may then draw five cards. He will try to arrange all or part of his cards to spell a word. As soon as one person can spell a word, he wins a point, and the game begins again. If no one can spell a word, then each player in turn may draw another card.

Keep track of your score on a piece of scrap paper. At the end of the playing time, the person with the most points is the winner.

3. BOOK REPORT FORMS (Grades 3-8)

A. Preparation and Materials: Mimeograph book-report forms similar to the example shown below.

Example:

```
            BOOK REPORT
   1.The name of the book is _____
   2.The author of the book is _____
   3.The book tells about _____
   _____
   _____
   _____
   4.The part I like best is_____
```

B. Introduction to the Class: Many of you have been reading books in your free time. I have placed on the free time table some forms you may use to keep a record of the books you read. Let's look at one of these forms together.

At the top you'll see a space for you to draw a

picture about the story. Under this are several sentences for you to complete. The first one says, "The name of the book is . . ." To finish this sentence, just write the name of the book.

The next one says, "The author of the book is . . ." You can find the author's name on the cover or the title page of the book. Write that name to finish this sentence.

The third one says, "This book tells about . . ." Here you might name some of the people in the story and tell a little about what happened.

The last sentence says "The part I liked best was . . ." Here you can tell about your favorite part of the story.

After you have finished your book report, you may put it in this folder on my desk. I will save them for you, and later we can fasten your reports together to make a book to take home.

(Or, handing in a report may be used as a requisite for adding a check or star by that child's name on an independent reading record chart which is displayed in the classroom. Or, the report might be displayed by the book which it reviews to encourage others to read the same book.)

4. VOCABULARY CHARTS (Grades 1-3)

A. Preparation and Materials: Use a full sheet of unruled newsprint. Label it "Our New Words," and on it list the special words needed for any unit being currently studied. Leave a space by each word for a picture. Cut drawing paper into proper-sized squares for these illustrations.

Example:

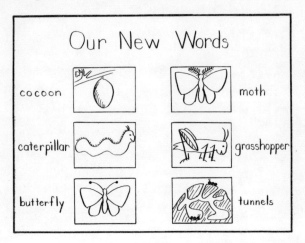

B. Introduction to the Class: In our study of insects (or whatever unit is currently being studied) we have come across many new words. We need to be able to read and spell these words to study about insects, but the words are very hard to remember.

To help you, I have made a chart with many of these hard words written on it. I have left a space by each word for a picture to show that word.

In your free time you may take one of these small squares of drawing paper, illustrate one of the listed words, and paste it on the chart where it belongs.

Then the next time you need one of these words in your reading or writing, you can use the chart to help you.

5. DAYS OF THE WEEK AND MONTHS OF THE YEAR (Grades 1-2)

A. Preparation and Materials: Make one set of flashcards showing the names of the days of the week, and another set showing the names of the months of the year. Put a rubber band around each complete set.

B. Introduction to the Class: I have placed two sets of flashcards on the free time table. One set has a card for the name of each day of the week. The other has a card for the name of each month of the year. We have been studying how to spell these words, and also how to name them in their proper order. You can practice with these cards.

For spelling, two of you may work together. One of you may hold one card at a time and tell your partner what word is written on it. Do not let him see the card. Ask him to spell the word. You may watch the card as he spells, and help him if he makes a mistake.

Or, one person could take one set of these cards and stand them up along the chalk tray in their proper order. Please shuffle the cards before you replace them on the free time table.

6. EXPERIENCE-READING CHART RACK (Grades 1-6)

A. Preparation and Materials: Prepare a chart rack as illustrated below. (Perhaps a parent would construct it, and children could paint it.)

Put two spring-type clothespins on a wire coat hanger. Wrap each end of the clothespins with adhesive tape so they will grip the charts more tightly. Hang one chart on each of these hangers.

Children can go to the rod during their free time and read any of the charts easily. Both sides of each chart can be used, for it can be viewed from either side.

Or one chart can easily be removed, hung over any convenient hook or nail in the room, and thus be readily available for review or reference.

Example:

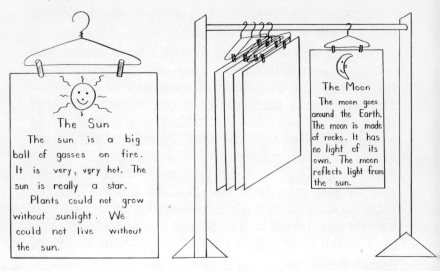

B. Introduction to the Class: Many of you may wish to use your free time to read some of the stories which are hung on our new chart rack. These are the stories we have written together while studying new science and social studies units.

You can push the charts along on the rack to make a space by the chart you wish to read. Then you can stand right in that space to read the chart.

7. READING READINESS (Grades Kdg.-1)
A. Preparation and Materials: Cut sixty 2-inch square cards. Choose ten simple designs, and make six cards showing each design.
Example:

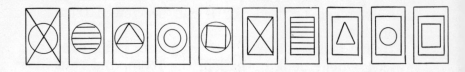

B. Introduction to the Class: In your free time, four of you together may play a game with these cards. First deal all of the cards. Each of you will have 15 cards. Then each child should put his cards face down in a pile in front of him.

Each of you then turn over your top card at the same time, so that everyone can see your card. If you see another card just like yours, say "Match." Then the child who has the card just like yours must give it to you. If no one has matching cards, you all turn over another card. This time the first child to say "Match" gets all the cards the other child has turned up.

The game is over when one child has no cards left. The person with the **most** cards is the winner. If you like, you may then shuffle the cards and begin a new game.

8. BEFORE AND AFTER (Grades 1-2)

Example:

		Q		
		R		
		S		
		T		
		U		
		V		

queen	toy	Sally	ride
pig	under	rabbit	very
umbrella	top	wagon	Susan

A. Preparation and Materials: Down the center of a Plymouth Chart (brand name) place cards showing consecutive letters of the alphabet. At the bottom of the chart put cards illustrating words beginning with letters which come before and after the letters placed above on the chart.

B. Introduction to the Class: Down the center of the Plymouth Chart, I have placed several letters of the alphabet. The first letter is "Q." What letter comes **before** "Q," Kathy? Yes, "P." Can you find a word at the bottom of the chart that starts with "P"? Yes, **pig.** Will you place **pig before** "Q" on the chart please, David?

What letter comes **after** "Q," class? Yes, "R." Can you find a word that starts with "R" and place it on the chart **after** "Q," Billy?

You may do the others in the same way. Put cards before and after each center letter to show words beginning with letters which come before and after that center letter.

Example:

wagon	V	umbrella
very	U	top
under	T	Susan
toy	S	rabbit
Sally	R	queen
ride	Q	pig

9. SPELLING PRACTICE (Grades 2-4)

A. Preparation and Materials: On the blackboard, write the week's spelling list. Set out chalk and an eraser.

B. Introduction to the Class: Some of you may wish to use your free time to practice writing your spelling words on the board.

The words for this week are listed on the board. You may use the space beside these words to practice writing the words themselves, or writing them in sentences.

Be sure to erase when you are finished so the board will be ready for the next person who wishes to use it.

APPENDIX I
"Magical e"
See Pages 19, 114, 175, 182, 183, 189, 191

The term "magical e" is used and described in STEPS TO MASTERY OF WORDS, a program in word analysis, published by Educational Service, Inc. The author of this series, Miss Nadine Fillmore, has graciously given us permission to quote from the Teacher's Guide Book, Three Star, page 59, in which she explains the "magical e" as follows:

"Since many pupils do not know the meaning of the word 'final' or the word 'silent,' it is best not to use the term 'final e' or 'silent e' with words such as **made, bite,** and **note.**

"As a result of reading fairy stories, most children understand the term 'magical' and are fascinated by it. The teacher explains that 'magical' means to make something change. The teacher writes these words on the board:

> (mad—made) — a is changed to a
>
> (bit—bite) — i is changed to i
>
> (cut—cute) — u is changed to u
>
> (not—note) — o is changed to o

"This change results from 'magical e' . . ."

APPENDIX II
Syllabification — See Pages 17, 145, 197 and 198

Helpful rules dividing words have been set forth in a clear, easy-to-teach manner by the author of STEPS TO MASTERY OF WORDS, Miss Nadine Fillmore. We appreciate her giving us permission to print the following extract from the Teacher's Guide, Three Star, pages 77-79. Publishers are Educational Service, Inc., P. O. Box 219, Stevensville, Michigan 49127.

SYLLABIFICATION OF BIG WORDS

"If the pupil is to enjoy reading and spelling, he must be able to divide words at sight, accurately and rapidly. While this ability to divide words is necessary, it should not be misused. Pupils should divide words only as a means to mastering a new word. If a pupil divides all words, his reading speed will be slow and his comprehension will be poor. The aim of this course is to give the pupil mastery over the simple rules for dividing words so that he will have this ability as a tool when he needs it in attacking new words. In STEPS TO MASTERY OF WORDS, the pupil gets practice in dividing words in Section 5-b of most units.

"The pupil is required to divide each word and to identify the rule used with each word. After dividing the new word, the pupil gets experience in using the word in a sentence and spelling the word. Through this procedure, many big words of each lesson become sight words for the pupil. The experience of dividing the big words is the first step to mastering the word, but once the pupil knows the word, he should not be permitted to divide it.

"Finding the 'beginning' of the word is the most important phase of syllabification. For this reason, the author has explained in detail the 5 rules which the pupil should know for selecting the letters of the first division. If the pupil knows the 'beginning' of the word, which is the first division, he can usually pronounce the rest of the word. However, he should know how to accurately divide the remaining part of the word.

"The rules for dividing a word are:

RULE A

"A word has as many divisions as it has vowel sounds.

"The following words cannot be divided because they have only 1 vowel sound:

> "jump" has 1 vowel sound and 1 division
> "sand" has 1 vowel sound and 1 division
> "bench" has 1 vowel sound and 1 division
> "hunt" has 1 vowel sound and 1 division

"The following words have 2 vowel sounds and 2 divisions: 'rob-in,' 'sev-en,' 'cab-in.' These words have 3 vowel sounds and 3 divisions: 'con-duc-tor,' 'hos-pit-al,' 'car-pen-ter.'

"Words may have as many as 4 or 5 divisions if they have that many vowel sounds.

"Silent vowels do not count in making a division of a word. Examples are: "Val-en-tine" has 4 vowels but only 3 vowel sounds. The Magical "e" in this word is silent and does not count in making another division of the word. 'Tip-toe' has two vowel sounds. The Magical "e" is silent and does not make another divison.

" 'Sun-shine' has 2 vowel sounds. The Magical 'e' is silent and does not make another division of the word.

" 'Sea-son' has 3 vowels, but only 2 vowel sounds. The letter 'a' is silent.

" 'Mail-man' has 3 vowels, but only 2 vowel sounds. The letter 'i' is silent.

"The pupils apply these rules in Section 5-b of most units in My Word Study Book. This practice will equip the pupils to divide new words automatically when they encounter them in reading.

RULE B

"The first division of the word is at the beginning of the word.

"The pupil will soon learn that there are five possibilities for the beginning of the word. They are called rules 1, 2, 3, 4, and 5. The rules and examples which follow are given for the teacher's convenience.

RULE 1

"In a compound word, the first word is usually the first division.

"(A compound word is a word which is made from two other words.)

Examples are:

birth-day	neck-tie
mail-man	tooth-brush
sun-set	rain-bow
milk-man	pop-corn
bath-tub	drug-store

"The first word of these compound words is the first division. The two words found in each compound word can easily be found on the Sound Chart.

"It will help the pupil to remember Rule 1 by associating the 'first word' with the 'first division" of the word — the '1's' go together.

RULE 2

"If a word begins with a vowel (a-i-u-o-e), the first division is usually the letters for the first 2 sounds.

in-vite	at-tic	or-chard
1 2	1 2	1 2
es-cape	in-vent	ac-tor
1 2	1 2	1 2
ar-tist	ad-vise	um-pire
1 2	1 2	1 2

"These words begin with vowels, and the first division is the letters for the first 2 sounds. The teacher will impress upon the pupils that Rule 2 goes with the letters for the first 2 sounds. The two number "2's" go together.

RULE 3

"If a word begins with a consonant, the first division is usually the letters for the first 3 sounds.

Examples:

rob-in	sat-in	lem-on
123	123	1 2 3
sev-en	vis-it	hab-it
123	123	123
cab-in	pic-nic	tab-let
123	123	123

"Pupils can pronounce most words correctly by knowing the 'beginning' of the word. As Rule 3 is used most often in syllabification of unknown words, encourage the pupil to say to himself, "What are the letters for the first three sounds?"

RULE 4

"If a word begins with a prefix, the first division is usually the prefix.

"The most important prefixes are 'a-be-de-re-ex' and are printed in red ink on the upper left-hand corner of the Sound Chart. Examples are:

a-bout	be-tween	de-fend	ex-act
a-gree	be-gan	de-mand	ex-pense

RULE 5

"If a word begins with a consonant, followed by a vowel that says its own letter name, the first division is usually the letters for the first 2 sounds.

"Teacher Note: Rule 5 is seldom used. Instruct the pupils to always try the letters for the first 3 sounds for the first division. If the word does not have meaning with the letters for first 3 sounds as the first division, then try the letters for the first 2 sounds.

"The pupil sees the new word 'paper.' As he does not know the word, he tries Rule 3 which is: "If a word begins with a consonant, the first division of the word is usually the letters for the first 3 sounds." Therefore, he would try the word as "pap-er." As the word has no meaning when pronounced this way, he tries Rule 5, which is: "If a word begins with a consonant, followed by a vowel which is long, the first division is the letters for the first 2 sounds." He now arrives at the correct pronunciation of the word, which is "pa-per." Other examples are: "music" which has no meaning with Rule 3— "mus-ic" so he tries Rule 5, which gives him "mu-sic."
1 2

"razor," which has no meaning with Rule 3—"raz-or," so he tries Rule 5, "ra-zor."
1 2

"pupil," which has no meaning with Rule 3—"pup-il," so he tries Rule 5, "pu-pil."
1 2

"bacon," which has no meaning with Rule 3—"bac-on," so he tries Rule 5, "ba-con."
1 2

"If a word begins with a consonant, the pupil should always try Rule 3, then try Rule 5."

"The pupils will soon recognize 'twin letters' in a word. When a letter is repeated in a word so that the letters stand together, they are called 'Twin Letters,' with each twin letter standing in a separate division. The second twin letter is silent.
Examples are:

lesson	les-son	puppet	pup-et
	1 2 3		1 2 3
bonnet	bon-net	rabbit	rab-bit
	1 2 3		1 2 3
ribbon	rib-bon	cotton	cot-ton
	1 2 3		1 2 3
kitten	kit ten	button	but-ton
	1 2 3		1 2 3

"NOTE: Letters which blend together to make one sound are counted as one sound. Examples are:

blan-ket (the blend "bl" counts as 1 sound)
1 2 3

trac-tor (the blend "tr" counts as 1 sound)
1 2 3

prob-lem (the blend "pr" counts as 1 sound)
1 2 3

plat-form (the blend "pl" counts as 1 sound)
1 2 3

drag-on (the blend "dr" counts as 1 sound)
1 2 3

"The teacher will impress upon the pupil that Rule 3 goes with the letters for the first 3 sounds. The two number "3's" go together.

The teacher will explain that Rule 3 is used for finding the first division more often than any other.

"The pupils should be instructed to apply Rule 3 to a strange word that has only one vowel sound, even though a word with one vowel sound cannot be divided. Examples are:

mail grain (the blend "gr" counts as 1 sound)
1 2 3 1 2 3

road float (the blend "fl" counts as 1 sound)
1 2 3 1 2 3

pool broom (the blend "br" counts as 1 sound)
1 2 3 1 2 3

coin spoil (the blend "sp" counts as 1 sound)
1 2 3 1 2 3

barn smart (the blend "sm" counts as 1 sound)
1 2 3 1 2 3

bird third (the blend "th" counts as 1 sound)
1 2 3 1 2 3

heat wheat (the blend "wh" counts as 1 sound)
1 2 3 1 2 3

loud cloud (the blend "cl" counts as 1 sound)
1 2 3 1 2 3

- -

See over for Order Blank

Cut on dotted line, and mail to

EDUCATIONAL SERVICE, INC.
P. O. Box 219
Stevensville, Michigan 49127

Ideas for All Levels Through Grade 8

SPICE   CREATE

PROBE   ACTION

PLUS   STAGE

SPARK   RESCUE

ANCHOR

For Quicker Lesson Planning

The above books all contain practical and simple games, ideas and activities that will arouse the elementary student's desire to learn.

(CUT ON LINE)

I wish to place the following order:

- ☐ SPICE @ 4.60 (Language Arts)
- ☐ PROBE @ 4.60 (Science)
- ☐ PLUS @ 4.60 (Arithmetic)
- ☐ SPARK @ 4.60 (Social Studies)
- ☐ CREATE @ 4.60 (Art)
- ☐ ACTION @ 4.60 (Physical Activities)
- ☐ STAGE @ 4.60 (Dramatics)
- ☐ RESCUE @ 4.60 (Remedial Reading)
- ☐ ANCHOR @ 4.60 (Vocabulary Discovery)

Individual Orders under $5.00 must be accompanied by payment.
30-Day Money-Back Guarantee.

Your Name _____

Your Address _____
STREET OR BOX NUMBER

_____
CITY   STATE   ZIP

Name of School and Grade _____